PSYCHIC
&EMPATH
ABILITIES

SARAH
STONE

TABLE OF CONTENTS

INTRODUCTION

S ome people are born with the ability to predict or influence random events, such as a card player being dealt a certain hand. Some people have the "feeling" that something is about to happen. This article will explore why psychic and empath abilities are so common and what can be done with them.

Our brains are constantly trying to collect and synthesize information from our external environment. There is an innate need to pay attention, that's just one of the ways our brains protect us from danger. As we proceed through our lives, our brains become better at dealing with the information coming from our environment. It is a survival trait that, when combined with the 'natural' tendency to move toward what attracts us and away from what repulses us, helps us survive.

There is a considerable amount of brain processing power and energy used by our mind to do this "information filtering." We also have to stay positive about this process so that we don't get overwhelmed or stressed. If our brains are constantly bombarded with "information" and we don't know how to deal with it, it gets very hard to live comfortably in society. We need to be able to filter out the majority of the information we receive but also be able to accept new ideas without questioning them too much.

A person with psychic abilities or an empath is someone who has a brain that is not in balance. In a normally functioning brain, there is an ongoing balance between attraction and repulsion, empathy and personal boundaries, desire and actions. When that balance is disturbed in certain individuals, it can result in them being able to predict random events or being 'sensitive' to others' feelings or emotions. The reason for this imbalance is genetic makeup linked to our DNA but also influenced by environmental factors (like stressful life events).

Clairvoyance is an ability to see or sense events, objects, or people in places out of normal sensory contact, not yet in existence, as well as to perceive past or future events. It is assumed that clairvoyance requires the use of some level of Extrasensory Perception (ESP). Some people with clairvoyant abilities can help find lost objects or missing persons. This happens when they "see" the person while they are looking for them, usually by receiving visual images that allow them to locate them. Sometimes a person's appearance may also be a clue to their current location.

Psychometry is an ability to perceive or "feel" through physical contact with objects, people, places, or an event in the past. It is mostly used by people that possess ESP in terms of premonition, clairvoyance, and healing. This happens when they send their minds to explore the object and pick up memories from thousands of years ago passed down from their ancestors. These memories appear as visions when reinserted into the object.

Precognition is the ability to detect events occurring many years ahead during a person's lifetime (even before conception). It is only used by certain individuals that also possess ESP. This ability is thought to be the result of the brain being unable to process certain information received from the future. This happens when they can "see" past events as if they were happening right now in front of them.

Telepathy is the ability to exchange thoughts, feelings, or emotions over a distance without using any signals (including sounds) for communication. It is thought that this ability comes about due to the brain being unable to filter out too much of its environment. This happens when a person's mind and the minds of others are so similar that messages become clear.

PART 1: EMPATH

CHAPTER 1
WHAT DOES IT MEAN TO BE AN EMPATH?

Most people have some ability to read others and notice subtle behavioral nuances that clue them into how a person is feeling. For instance, if you go out to lunch with your best friend and notice that they are not talking much, you can determine that your best friend is feeling sad or bothered by something. They are not the typical talkers, so you realize that something must be going on.

However, an empath's ability not only to read people but to take in people's energies is much more complex.

Lipps also produced a theory that the inner imitation of others was central to the existence of empathy between humans. Besides, philosopher Martin Buber contextualized the concept of empathy's existence in human-to-human relationships as "I and Thou," as opposed to "I and It," which would show a lack of sympathy (Riess, 2017).

Buber's simple yet profound description of human relationships proves how "humane respect and concern for the other is contrasted with objectification and dehumanization of another person, which is in evidence too often in today's societies"

(Reiss, 2017). This is a major reason that empaths play an important role in the world, and how understanding empaths and empathy can help start the healing process.

Often, empaths are confused with highly sensitive people (HSP). Learning the vocabulary can help you decide where you fall. A highly sensitive person is exactly what they sound like. Common characteristics of a highly sensitive person include experiencing emotions more intensely than the average person, taking criticism poorly, taking things more personally than most people would, struggling to make decisions, meticulousness, and introversion. Of course, these characteristics vary from person to person—even within the HSP subgroup. Empaths share a lot of characteristics with highly sensitive people, which is why they are so commonly misrepresented as identical.

Some of these shared character traits include sensitivity to stimuli, taking a long time to unwind at the end of the day (this is typical because of the mental toll that the person's sensitivity to various stimuli throughout the day takes on them both emotionally and physically), being emotionally intelligent and able to read a person's body language more efficiently than the average person, and exhibiting the desire to help those around them.

Empaths often exhibit all the qualities of highly sensitive people but on a more intense level. The clearest example of this is the empath's ability to absorb external energies that are typically subtler than the average person would notice.

Empaths can absorb these subtle energies from people or places. For instance, an empath might enter a house with a dark past and feel physically ill due to the subtle ill-natured aura within the environment. The empath might experience this reaction subtly or intensely (again, every empath's experience varies from person to person, and individual experiences do not discount the empath's credibility or abilities).

An empath's emotional intuition is typically much more intense than a highly sensitive person would be, as empaths can notice subtler energies and absorb those energies from surrounding people and environments that a highly sensitive person would not perceive typically.

All empaths are highly sensitive people, but not all are necessarily empaths. If you're wondering where you fall, you can start by asking yourself a few questions. For starters, are you someone who is easily affected by external emotional stimuli? This can be anything from minor inconveniences that ruin your day to a pattern of falling in love much quicker than others when you start dating someone. These are characteristics of highly sensitive people.

Now, take one step further. Do you fall in love with people easily because you feel highly connected to them? Do you feel that you somehow understand their thoughts and emotions so thoroughly that when you are together, you mold into one person? This is a sign that you might be an empath. If this is the case, then you are absorbing your partner's emotional energy, thereby making it appear as though it is part of your own.

On the other hand, many highly sensitive people report heightened physical experiences of their 5 senses. For instance, being in the same room as someone wearing a strong, chemical-smelling perfume will become a major ordeal for a highly sensitive person. This description is that of the HSP, and not necessarily specific to the empath.

Do you find that you need alone time to recharge? This is the case for most HSPs and empaths; the difference is that HSPs experience this longing for alone time because it takes them a long time to transition into a calm state from the hustle and bustle of social life. Due to their sensitivity to external stimuli, they often feel overwhelmed during the day.

On the other hand, empaths tend to need alone time to recharge after socialization because they are drained from absorbing the energies of external stimuli (mostly from other people), and they need to be away from people to focus on harnessing their energy, as opposed to taking in all these different energies at once and dealing with the challenges that come.

It comes down to figuring out whether you are absorbing energies from others. Can you feel what others are feeling, as though these feelings are your own? Can you notice subtler energies that aren't obvious to other people? These are signs that you are an empath.

Empaths and highly sensitive people exist on a spectrum, just as everyone. At one end of the empathic spectrum are sociopaths and psychopaths, who show extremely limited-to-no empathy for others. A sociopath is a person with a psychological antisocial personality disorder that severely limits their control over behavior and moral conscience. Common traits of sociopaths include compulsive lying and impulsive behavior without regard for potential consequences. Similar to a sociopath, a psychopath is a person with a psychological disorder that severely limits emotional response, empathy, and control over behavior. A psychopath may additionally appear to be antisocial or violent.

These are followed by narcissists, highly sensitive people, and finally empaths. A narcissist is a person who shows and prioritizes extreme self-involvement. Most people fall somewhere between narcissists and highly sensitive people—although these types of individuals are common.

There are certain characteristics that empaths exhibit that HSPs do not exhibit at all. One of these characteristics is an empath's ability to unconsciously mimic other people's experiences as they go through certain emotional states. There are 2 ways in which the empath exhibits this ability; the first one being the mirroring of someone else's physical motions. Neuroscientists have studied regions in the brain where mirroring takes place. This brain function is strong in the empath and, therefore, translates to the empath physically mirroring another person's corporal activity, whether mimicking their facial expressions, their mannerisms, their gait, or small actions as they are performing a task. This would occur subconsciously in the empath's brain, without the empath realizing that they are mirroring the person that they are looking at.

If, for instance, an empath is watching their mother cook as they sit at the kitchen counter, and their mother's hand accidentally makes contact with the hot stove, the onlooking empath might quickly pull their hand back as their mother does instinctively to remove it from the heat. The empath exhibits instinctive motor and sensory reactions as if it were their hand that had touched the hot stove.

In the same way, the empaths imitate the mannerisms and facial expressions to a greater degree than individuals who are unemphatic. Patients unconsciously mimic others' actions and facial expressions via brain mechanisms that mirror them by stimulating the same motor and sensory areas in the observers' brains. This mirroring ability has been proven at the level of single muscle fibers. For example, if a person's hand muscle is pricked by a fine needle, then the same motor and sensory areas are activated in the observer's brain.

The second way that empaths can mimic other people's experiences is through emotions. This characteristic is the most discussed trait of the empath, as shared emotions are what typically comes to mind when someone thinks of empaths. Like an empath might mirror the physicality of another person whom they are watching, the empath also tends to mirror the emotions of close people. If an empath's mother has just burned her hand on a hot stove and has seriously hurt herself but wants to hide the pain from her child, then she might stifle an outward reaction to being burned. However, an empath would nevertheless know exactly what their mother is feeling, as they would feel the same emotions, just from seeing subtle cues from their mother. This happens when the empath's brain creates the same signals as their mother's brain after the burn. Therefore, the empath is not simply perceiving their mother's emotional state, but they are experiencing the same emotional state themselves.

CHAPTER 2
HOW TO RECOGNIZE IF YOU ARE AN EMPATH?

As social beings that are dependent on social interactions and emotional connections among us, we all experience and possess the feeling of empathy toward others, only varying in degree from person to person. We may relate to it as kindness, and almost all of us strive to become a person who is kind, who cares about and considers the feelings of other people. Empathy is, as defined by Webster's New World Dictionary, "a feeling, emotional or intellectual identification with another." The ability to understand the experiences and feelings of others outside of an individual's perspective is known as empathy.

For example, say that your friend is going through a loss in the family. In such a scenario, it is empathy that allows you to understand the pain that your friend is going through and the emotions that she is dealing with, even if the situation and the circumstances are completely different from where you stand and what you are feeling. However, that is not all. As an empath, you take all of this a little further. An empath senses and feels these emotions that the other person is feeling as though it is their very own. If we explain it in simpler words, it can be said that as an empath, someone else's pain, happiness, or anger becomes your pain, happiness, and anger. Empaths are hypersensitive people who can understand, feel, tune in to, and resonate with the feelings of others around them. This can happen voluntarily, but sometimes, this becomes the case even involuntarily.

What Is a Psychic Empath?

While all of us strive and work to become a better version of ourselves filled with kindness and understanding of those around us, some people are born with abilities beyond the normal kindness we know. Such people can connect and resonate with the emotions and feelings of other people on a very deep and powerful level that is beyond normal capabilities. Do you often feel an instant connection with the feelings and emotions of other people around you, like your friends and family, even when you are in a very different emotional state altogether? Let's dive into what psychic empathy truly is, how it works, and what it means. This will help you recognize and understand your nature and abilities.

Empathy, as discussed earlier, is the ability to identify, understand, and feel sympathy toward the feelings of other people. The term psychic empath is derived from empathy itself and is used quite frequently to refer to a psychic individual who is intensely sensitive and receptive to other people's feelings, emotions, and energies that they experience all these emotions as though it is their own. The term psychic empath is becoming more popular and common in the psychic and paranormal realms. This is because psychic empaths can probe deeply into the soul of another person and help them identify and experience the feelings and emotions that may have been blocked. They display profound sensitivity to the emotional states of both themselves and others. Having said that, sometimes, it is even possible that the emotional states of others may overpower their own emotions as they are barely able to distinguish their feelings from someone else. There is always a probability that the empaths themselves are not aware of their abilities and may just refer to it as being super sensitive around others.

There is a distinct difference between what empathy is and what psychic empathy is, and it is very important not to get these 2 confused. Empathy is a human emotion that exists in all of us in varying degrees, and we can connect and sympathize with people and their feelings. Psychic empaths, on the other hand, have an extrasensory perception that is above normal human empathy. Psychic empaths can easily detect and identify the feelings and emotions of people around them, and they can pick these up on non-visual, non-verbal cues. They just know what people are going through and the emotions they are feeling regardless of the fact whether that person is letting out his/her feelings at all or not. Therefore, they feel the moods, intentions, and motives of others unconsciously. Some psychic empaths can even feel the emotional impact that is radiated by people, animals, and plants in the surrounding environment and even the universe. While everybody who has healthy emotional states can feel empathy, psychic empaths can experience the emotions of others directly.

In addition to that, a psychic empath also differs distinctly from a traditional psychic as the former cannot sense, see, hear, or read into the spiritual realm or get glimpses of the future possibilities; rather, they can read and identify emotions. They can instantly enter into another person's aura. They can connect to the feelings and emotions the other person is feeling deeply and understand their life experiences almost instantly and very intimately. However, similar to other psychic abilities, an individual may be born with it, and this ability is often known to be multi-generational. But it is believed that a person might be able to obtain this ability after a near-death experience. This is not a confirmed statement open to debate, but this is widely believed.

Are You a Psychic Empath?

Do you exhibit strong empathetic tendencies? Do you feel the emotions that are oddly not even connected to your own life? Were you able to relate to any of the extraordinary abilities of psychic empaths that we discussed above? If yes, chances are you might be one. To make sure whether or not you are one, you must try to separate your thoughts, emotions, and feelings from what you perceive from others. By doing so, you will be able to differentiate your feelings. That way, you will be in a better position to make sure whether or not you are functioning in an individual capacity or from information, emotions, and feelings that you have been perceiving.

Here are a few questions that you might want to ask yourself:

- Do you gain the knowledge and understanding about other people without being said anything, on a deeper and more accurate level, to be just a coincidence?

- Do you experience Deja Vu regularly?

- Do you find yourself avoiding and neglecting your feelings while you practice emotional labor on behalf of others?

- Do you find yourself reacting more strongly than anyone else in the room when it comes to emotional situations and topics?

Most psychic empaths do not realize their abilities and their full extent. Sometimes, they do not even realize they are psychic. Psychic empaths have shared that most of them grew up differently, feeling weird and like they did not fit in with people around them. The heightened sensitivity that they experience may have led to intense interactions with other people. If you are still not sure but feel like you have a very high degree of empathy than others, below are some common signs you might be a psychic empath.

Signs You Might Be a Psychic Empath

It is important to note that all of the following signs may not be relatable to all empaths as we all know by now empaths differ and have different abilities.

However, here are some most common signs that affirm you as an empath:

- Avoid intense situations that may result in a conflict.

- Extreme shyness, nervousness, anxiety in places and situations that are crowded.

- Always sought out by people for help or to listen to their problems whenever they are in trouble as they are good listeners and great counselors.

- Can tell if someone is lying or not being honest.

- Avoid public places and social encounters pretty often.

- Getting attached to animals and/or children easily.

- Sensitive to criticism and getting hurt easily.

- Feeling a sense of responsibility toward other people and helping them in pain and suffering — empaths perceive emotions very quickly and deeply.

- Getting attached emotionally to characters from movies, novels, etc., and being able to relate to their emotions as though they are real.

- Loving the beautiful harmony music offers. Tendency to drift away while listening to music because it means the opposite of chaos.

- Self-isolating oneself because it is difficult to be close to others, and you need time to heal and separate yourself from the emotions of the people around you.

- Your gut feelings and hunches are never wrong.

Once you have confirmed that you are a psychic empath, it becomes very important that you practice some coping strategies and learn to protect yourself and your feelings, as sometimes the pieces of information and feelings that you perceive become so much that it overloads and it will be very difficult to handle. You mustn't lose your true feelings and emotions in the sea of emotions that come toward you. However, with practice and patience, psychic empathy is a gift that will help you help others.

How to Deal with Being a Psychic Empath?

Being a psychic empath and having to deal with others' emotions, whether positive or negative, is very difficult. Some empaths even go to extreme lengths to numb the emotions they are perceiving. Therefore, it is crucial to have constructive ways and coping mechanisms to deal with the gift.

- Whenever you are around unpleasant and negative people and sensations, visualize a shield that is fluid to separate yourself from them and their emotions.

- Practice meditation and yoga regularly to cleanse your thoughts, feelings, and emotions, as well as release stress.

- Eat nutritious meals as empaths are sensitive people and are affected by the food they put into their bodies. If you eat unhealthy things, you may feel terrible. Eat well to be physically and mentally strong.

- Give yourself a lot of alone time and in that time, allow yourself to recharge, do things that you love and enjoy, and heal away from the interference of others.

- Focus on the positive and absorb as much positive energy as you can. Make a list of all the good things you have done with the gift given to you to look at when you feel overwhelmed or go out into nature and absorb nature's positive energy and channel the negative energy.

As you have seen, being empathetic is what makes you human but not a psychic empath. A psychic empath feels these feelings beyond normal perception, and there are several different empaths. If you have made sure that you are an empath, consider talking to other empaths, be patient and practice your abilities. This gift provides you with wonderful opportunities to help others, but make sure to understand your limitations and take care of yourself.

CHAPTER 3
7 TYPES OF EMPATHS

Some psychic empaths can sense the emotions and how others are feeling by tapping into their aura or energetic vibrations, while others, on the other hand, can use a unique ability known as "Claircognition" to simply "know" the emotions and the underlying feelings of a person without having any obvious verbal, vision, or any type of clue. If you feel like you can instantly connect to someone's feelings on a personal and deep level and even feel very overwhelmed when you are in a crowd full of people due to their emotions draining your energy, you might be a psychic empath yourself. From empaths who are physical to emotional empaths, from earth empaths to animal empaths, there are several types of empaths present. These differences come forward due to the different types of ways through which they obtain information. Each one of these empaths has distinct abilities.

Here are the main and most common types of psychic empaths that may help you recognize which one is you:

1. Emotional Empath
As depicted by the name, these types of psychic empaths

experience the emotions of others. It does not matter whether or not the people in question are related to these empaths or not. They may feel the sorrow of a fellow passenger who has just lost his pet, the excitement of someone on the street who has just passed the interview, or the joy of the family that is expecting. These emotions do not necessarily have to be exhibited to be felt by the emotional empath; they just feel these emotions even if they are well hidden inside by these people.

However, as shown in the example above, this ability has both pros and cons, as the empath may suffer the pain of someone who is suffering while they can also rejoice in the joy of someone else. This type of empath may feel emotionally drained by the negative and narcissistic emotions that they may feel as the day goes on. For example, the emotions of people who suffer from low self-esteem and always find themselves in crisis mode, seeking constant validation and reassurance can negatively impact the emotional well-being of the empath as well.

2. Physical Empath

Physical empaths can experience the physical ailments of those around them. They respond to the physical symptoms and actions of people around them. Therefore, when someone is laughing or crying and expressing their emotions physically, the physical empath is most likely to mirror these actions regardless of whether you are experiencing these emotions yourself. Likewise, if you are around people who are suffering from illness or having some kind of body ache, you might experience similar discomfort as them. This ability has many negative impacts on the well-being of the empath as it is noticeably not delightful to experience the physical pain of someone. Hospitals prove to be a dreadful place to these empaths, as this generally happens when they are in the vicinity of injured people. However, in some cases, this can occur even across the further distance between the empath and the sufferer.

Due to all these negative impacts and effects, it becomes very important for the empath to train and concentrate on coping mechanisms. This is a major problem surrounding the physical empaths as they unconsciously manifest the physical symptoms of others onto themselves; therefore, it is important and helpful that they are surrounded by healthy and happy people most of the time so that these negative effects are set off. Another very important strategy that might help you if you identify yourself with one of these types of empaths is that you should set healthy boundaries with people and learn that it is okay to say "no" to spending time with people who will add to your stress levels.

3. Claircognizant Empath

These types of empaths can identify and understand the true nature of any given situation or thing. They can instantly recognize when someone is lying or is misleading, and similarly, they always just know the truth without any logical base. Not only that, they can know what is to be done and what is important in any situation. Due to this profound ability, the claircognizant empaths are the ideal people to turn to whenever faced with a crisis. The hallmark characteristic of this psychic ability is the empathetic ability to feel relaxed and at peace even when they face a crisis.

4. Earth Empath

Earth empaths are those who are in tune with nature and the environment. They possess the ability to feel and connect to the world and the universe as a whole. For instance, a forest fire can cause them to feel pain, and further, they can sense earthquakes and severe storms even before it happens. These can come as physical symptoms. These symptoms and the sensations they feel before a natural calamity depend on the empath themselves and the disaster that is making its way. As an outcome of feeling and resonating with the earth, they feel calm, relaxed, and at peace after the disaster has passed. Earth empaths rejoice in being outdoors amongst nature, and they thrive when they experience the miracles of nature and are among the natural energy sources. Earth empaths get energized when they see a beautiful sunrise, waterfalls, and other natural beauties. However, the negative impacts of pollution and environmental toxins can cause detrimental effects to them that are heightened than other normal human beings.

5. Intuitive Empath

Similar to emotional empaths, intuitive empaths also connect to the feelings and emotions of the people around them. However, there is more to that in these types of empaths as not only do they pick up on the emotions of others, but they also can see what truly lies underneath the feelings and emotions on the surface. They go beyond these emotions to see what lies underneath. They sense what is being hidden, unspoken, and not expressed. Most of the time, this type of empath also can understand whether a person is being truthful or is lying. Intuitive empaths are hence, good judges of character who can find out when someone is not being honest and, therefore, can find out the reality and truth in every situation.

6. Plant Empath

Just as emotional and physical empaths can connect to other people and their feelings, plant or flora empaths are known to form similar connections with plants. They are always in tune with the flora around them, such as the trees, flowers, etc. They are said to even be able to communicate with the plants, can hear their thoughts, and understand them. Therefore, they always know what a plant needs to be healthy. Not only that, as they are one with the flora around them, they have the ability of healing and herbalism. Not only do they communicate with plants, but this spiritual connection can also be carried to form human connections.

7. Animal Empath

Also known as the fauna empaths, they can connect to animals similar to flora empaths. They connect to their energy and can sense whether the animal is happy, sad, in pain, or suffering. They can hear and understand the thoughts of animals and even make their thoughts understood.

However, sometimes an animal empath's ability to connect and sense the animals' energy is only connected to one species of animals, for reasons unknown. It can be a terrible experience for animal empaths to be in or around places like a zoo where the animals are captivated and sometimes even abused. They cannot tolerate any violence or cruelty to animals and are very sensitive about it.

CHAPTER 4
THE 11 TRAITS OF
AN EMPATH

A review of the types of empaths gives the reader a sense of some of the traits that they possess. In this chapter, we think of an empath's traits as tendencies that empaths have in terms of their daily lives and interactions with others rather than specific "powers." We all know that they are sensitive people, but that sensitivity manifests in various ways. Here, those women and men ask if they may be an empath and develop a better sense of their truth by comparing these qualities to those that they possess. These traits also will give the reader a sense of how empaths can fall victim to the narcissist, which is itself a trait.

1. Feeling the Emotions

The trademark ability of the empath is their capacity to feel the emotions of others. Empaths do not merely possess sympathy, that is, the ability to feel compassion and tolerance for others, but they experience the subjective emotional states and experiences of others. They share the emotions of others almost as soon as they occur. This fascinating ability helps influence the other abilities of the empath though it can also be problematic (as you will see shortly).

2. Highly-Sensitive

The empath is not able to control their sensitivity to the things around them. In addition to their sensitivity to people, the empath may also experience sensitivity to things. They feel physical pain or sadness when they watch a sad or moving film. They may become enveloped in tears. For this reason and others, the empath is described as highly-sensitive by others (which they are).

3. Overwhelmed by Negativity

Because an empath feels things almost instantaneously, they can be overwhelmed when they are surrounded by negativity. It can be difficult for the empath to be around one negative or depressive person, but being in a group of such people can be deadening for them. This ability to be overwhelmed by a perception of emotion can cause the empath to avoid certain situations or people.

4. Introverted

Although the empath naturally forms connections with other people and generally derives pleasure from doing so, the empath tends to be an introvert. Although some think of introverts as "loner types," they are sensitive people who are on a sort of psychic-emotional journey. One therapist has described introverts as people who have extremely active brains that are weighed down by their thoughts.

5. Strong Intuitive Sense

The empath is strongly intuitive. They will have a "sense" of people, places, and things that guides their actions and interactions. The empath may be able to tell when another person is lying, whether another person is dangerous or a good individual, or whether they should avoid certain places. These intuitive perceptions also serve to heighten the introverted nature of the empath.

6. Low Pain Tolerance

The empath is sensitive in general, and this includes being sensitive to pain. Physical sensations that are mild or tolerable to others may be completely intolerable to the empath. Pain is one of those sensations that can be difficult. This perception is intensified in the empath because they tend to feel things with their entire body. Pain, therefore, becomes a sensation that is not localized to its source but is felt throughout the physical form of the empath.

7. Difficulty with Images of Pain or Horror Movies

Empaths will tend to avoid images of pain or violence because of their sensitivity. Recall that an empath feels the subjective states of others, and that can even include characters that they see on a television screen or in a movie theater. Even images of war in a magazine can trigger an empath. Such sensations can be isolating to an empath as the world can be filled with rough images though the empath often learns to manage them.

8. Attuned to Your Own Body

Because the empath has a high-powered antenna, they tend to be closely attuned to how their body feels. This means that physical symptoms can be intensified in the empath, or have psychic or psychological implications that are not present in other people.

9. You Feel the Ailments

When someone is dealing with an illness, the empath can feel it. Even an empath sitting in the waiting room of a doctor's office can find themselves feeling this person's complaint at one moment and then another person's shortly after. They can feel stomach pains if someone in the waiting room has a stomach complaint, joint pains, or if someone has arthritis. The complaint can take many forms.

10. Attuned to Other's Dishonesty

Empaths might want to consider seeking employment with law enforcement or the Federal Bureau of Investigation because they are closely attuned to the truthfulness of others. This is an interesting talent that perhaps has to do with the ability of the empath to be sensitive to the many cues that others send. This trait can also represent a type of extrasensory perception that is not well understood.

11. You Are Weighed Down by the Problems of Others

This is a 2-part trait of empaths. On the one hand, the empath can be overwhelmed by the problems of others because they sense everything, but they also tend to be bombarded by others with their problems. Indeed, the empath may not be conscious of some of their abilities others frequently are. The sensitive nature of the empath can be easily recognizable and lead to others laying their problems at the feet of a sensitive soul.

CHAPTER 5

HOW TO MASTER AND DEVELOP THESE SKILLS ABILITIES?

Because of the nature of your empathic abilities, it is necessary to find ways to empower yourself. You need to show yourself as a powerful and positive person having meaning and purpose in your life.

Perhaps, you are facing difficulty to draw out the good in you, and all you are feeling right now is emotional pain. **Take these necessary steps to discover yourself:**

- Take steps to energize and empower yourself.

- We have already discussed some ways to balance the energies of your mind and body by honing in on the chakras and practicing yoga.

- Apply them and experience the results.

While these are more on the scientific side of things, some practical things are allowing you to occupy yourself and bring greater meaning to you as a person. There are ways you can come from under the cloud and receive healing from your pain.

Art therapy uses art for self-expression to bring awareness and understanding of emotions and what goes on in the mind.

Psychotherapy techniques seek to understand the workings of a person's mind through the use of artistic expression.

Art therapy is usually presided over or monitored by an art therapist trained in both the arts and psychology. The therapist knows how to bring both disciplines together to assess your mental state and refer the condition for treatment if necessary. You can use any form of art, especially one appealing to you.

Art therapy uses expressive arts, such as drawing, painting, modeling, and photography. Music is also used, allowing you to play the drums, sing, or dance. They can determine what you are trying to communicate in your drawing or painting. In addition, art will help you relieve the stress and tensions built up in you. One of the most wonderful benefits is the therapy helps boost your self-esteem.

How to Use Mirror Work?

How can you, the empath, master mirror work for a richer and more meaningful life. A few minutes a day is enough.

- First, select a time of day when you are free from distractions and can dialogue with yourself.

- Find a mirror in which you can see your face or the whole body.

- Look straight at yourself. Preferably let your eyes make contact with those in the mirror. Now, you are face to face with the person in the mirror. Are you seeing the pain the person is feeling?

- Start talking. As you breathe deeply, make an affirmation and tell the person in the mirror "I am loved." Perhaps you will say, "I have as much brightness in the world as the sun. I'm going to light up the world today." Repeat this like a song as you breathe deeply.

- Work on specific emotions. If you feel something like anger welling up and threatening to overwhelm you, use mirror work to turn your attention to the specific issue. Use your face to convey what you are feeling and speak to it. Call yourself by name as you address the person in the mirror (Learning self-love, 2016).

Each time you pass the mirror, glance at it and remind the person in it of the affirmation you made earlier.

A fairly new form of psychotherapy designed to assist in the healing of your emotional stress is EMDR — Eye Movement Desensitization and Reprocessing.

When a part of your body receives a wound, for example, its natural defenses work to heal the cut. If something should happen to the wound in the healing process, it becomes inflamed and causes pain.

Once you apply a healing solution to the wound, it closes, and the recuperation takes place. In the same way, when EMDR is applied to a mind that has undergone psychological trauma, the barrier many people have built over time disappears and mental health is restored.

EMDR has become one of the most successful forms of treating mental disorders stemming from psychological and physical trauma.

Indeed, studies have shown that 84-90% of post-traumatic stress disorder cases have received full recovery after only 90 minutes of EMDR sessions.

The results are even better if you are a single trauma case. You are more likely to enjoy 100% recovery after 50 minutes with the program (EMDR Institute, 2017).

You can readily see how you can benefit from EMDR. It can help you calm stress, soothe turmoil in your mind, and overcome feelings of powerlessness shadowing your life.

One patient disclosed how she had lived under a cloud of mental anguish for practically 50 years. She suffered the traumatic effects of childhood abuse and the tragedy involving her lifelong partner. Then, she discovered EMDR (Marshal, 2017).

How Does EMDR Work?

EMDR is an 8-step treatment plan. A clinical therapist uses eye movements or another form of stimulation to connect you to the distress you are facing. In doing so, the therapist lets you focus on the memory of the disturbing situation while moving a hand back and forth across your field of vision. You engage in eye movements similar to what takes place in REM sleep. As this transpires, you will start to process the event causing the distress, something you have failed to do on your own.

As an empath, NLP Reframing is good for you. Use this tool to restore balance and empower yourself. Reframe your experience to see the better side of it. See the situation as an opportunity for positive results. Do not let it control you.

To have a better idea, consider what Roger Ellerton says. During the 1984 presidential campaign, people expressed concern about Ronald Reagan's age. When asked about "the age issue," Reagan said, "I will not hold my opponent's youth and inexperience against him." The retort ended all conversation about his age for the rest of the campaign. Reagan went on to win the election convincingly.

We are all familiar with the expression, "When life gives you lemons, make lemonade." The classic reminds people to reframe their negative experiences as something positive.

You would agree you are in the right position to use NLP Reframing to bring some stability to your life.

CHAPTER 6
HOW TO GET RID OF STRESS AND NEGATIVE ENERGY?

The health of the empath can get compromised easily, especially if you are not doing anything to protect your energy and take time to recuperate after challenging experiences. At this point in your life, you are probably so used to dealing with everyone else's feelings that it feels normal, and taking a different approach doesn't occur to you.

The recovery process for an empath differs widely from person to person, but overall, it can feel like an endless cycle of ups and downs if you are not preventing yourself from getting too caught up in another person's distress. Here are some of the ways the empath's emotional and physical health can be compromised:

- Feelings of grief, melancholy, and depression.

- Tender and achy muscles, joints, and limbs.

- Common cold and allergy symptoms.

- Weakened immune system.

- Chronic neck, shoulder, and back pain.

- Insomnia.

- Undiagnosed physical or emotional pain is the result of absorbing too many people's toxic or negative energy.

- Symptoms are similar to chronic fatigue and autoimmune disorders.

- Paranoia.

- Anxiety and worry, sometimes chronically.

- Tiredness and exhaustion.

- Low self-esteem or low self-worth.

- Difficulty maintaining a healthy weight.

- Dysfunctional emotional bonds with other people that are repetitive and habitual.

- Alcohol or drug abuse.

- Addictions to food, substances, or entertainment, such as television or gambling.

- Difficulty putting personal problems aside.

- General feelings of fear about life; lack of security, and much more.

It might be hard to be certain that being an empath could lead to all of these problems and issues. The issue is not about being an empath; the issue is about not understanding your gift and learning the best methods for taking good care of your energy.

All too often, empaths are left without recourse and end up feeling one or several of the symptoms listed above. If you can understand the way our energy works, then you can understand why other people's feelings have such a volatile impact on an empath.

The human heart is electrical. It has energy radiating out from its center as far as 3 feet outside of your chest. Is that amazing?! Your heart is always emitting a force field of energy that can be affected by anyone you come into contact with. So, imagine that you are feeling happy, joyful, relaxed, and affectionate. Then all of a sudden, you come within 2 feet of someone angry, frustrated, rejected, and emotionally wounded. All of that energy is radiating out of their heart 2-3 feet outside of their body and coming into your sphere of energy.

A lot of people will not notice this energy, but an empath picks it up like a radio signal. Empaths have an antenna for these types of energies and pull them in like a tractor beam. And it's not just the energy at the heart level. Your body has multiple energy centers like the heart that are all working together to keep your emotional, physical, and mental energy in balance.

The empath may not be aware that it is happening when it does, but as soon as they come into contact with enough of those low emotions and negative feelings, they have just collected a whole lot of other people's distress, sorrow, and misfortune, sometimes without even talking to them.

When you have enough negative energy circulating in your universe of vibration and frequency, you disrupt your balance and end up dealing with a variety of symptoms that can lead to or look like the list above. Some of the more chronic issues build up slowly over time and many of them are the result of toxic partnerships and environmental conditions.

It helps to understand this idea and imagery so that you can be aware of how to protect yourself from other people's energy spheres. The more you collect, the harder it is to maintain good health. The more you learn to protect your energy and stop absorbing the energy of other people around you, the easier it becomes to stay balanced emotionally and physically.

The following techniques are designed to help you remain true to your empathic heart while connecting to your energy and staying grounded so that you don't absorb other people's emotional distress and baggage.

Grounding and Protecting Meditation

Grounding is a method that helps you connect your energy to the earth below your feet. Even if you are wearing shoes and you are on the 25th floor of a skyscraper, you can still ground your energy. The concept of it comes from how electrical wires are grounded to the soil or floor of a building to help redirect energy, or in this case, electricity, in case there is a short circuit somewhere in the wiring.

For people, who are also electrical current and vibrating frequencies, grounding is the same concept, allowing you to redirect your focus and energy to a more balanced state of affairs. If you are an Empath and you are in the midst of a lot of emotional energy, you can easily lose your footing and become ungrounded, leaving you vulnerable to the energies of others. The idea is that you keep grounding as a way of protecting your energy from taking on too much anyone or anything else.

The rules of grounding are simple:

1. Keep your focus on your energy.

2. Center yourself.

3. Maintain.

The energy of yourself can get lost in the dynamic forces of what's happening around you. Self-awareness isn't selfish, it's healthy and responsible. To stay grounded, you have to be aware of yourself. Centering yourself means holding that awareness and being able to freely exist in that nature. You don't have to be a statue. You can move and enjoy your expressiveness and personality. Centering means you get to practice being yourself while you remain grounded. Then, all you have to do is maintain that balance within yourself so that you can stay open and heartfelt with the people around you.

The following meditation is something you can perform in the morning before you leave the house, in the bathroom, at a restaurant, in your parked car, wherever you need it at the moment. It will only take a few moments and will help you feel secure in your energy as you move through your life experiences.

1. Begin by closing your eyes and taking a deep breath in. Inhale through the nose. Try to inhale for a count of 5-10.

2. Slowly exhale through the mouth for the same count as you inhaled.

3. Bring your hands together, either in your lap or in front of your heart. They can be palm to palm, or just touching — whatever works for the environment that you are in.

4. Take another deep inhale followed by an exhale.

5. With your feet on the ground, wherever you are, imagine a shaft of light coming out of the bottom of each foot, like the roots of a tree.

6. Picture the light getting long and going through the Earth's crust, pavement, or whatever floor of the skyscraper you are on so that it goes all the way to the center of the Earth (If you don't make it to the center, that's okay, as long as the light roots from your feet are going deep into the ground).

7. They can be a color, or they can simply be golden or white, depending on your personal preferences.

8. With your visual of these light roots penetrating the Earth, now see the energy of that light coming back from the Earth, up through your feet and into your body, through your heart, and out of the crown of your head. You still want to see the light connecting deeply into the Earth.

9. Sit in this posture for several inhales and exhales. See all of your being connected deeply to the Earth and feel that earth energy coming back up through you and filling your body.

10. When you feel grounded and protected, you can open your eyes and move forward with your day.

This meditation is very simple and only takes a few minutes of your time. It can help you rebalance yourself after a distressing moment or an intense conversation with a difficult person. When you connect to your energy and ground it to the Earth, you are permitting yourself to exist, take up space, and return to your center so that you don't lose yourself in the sea of other people's energies.

I had personally used this before a business meeting and after, during an airplane ride (and the beams of light from my feet had to go all the way down from 30,000 feet in the air to connect to the planet), and in a hospital before a procedure. I have heard of others using this meditation in their cars in parking lots after getting out of a busy shopping center, in the bathroom at an office party, and during childbirth.

It is a very simple and versatile tool and uses creative visualization to help you connect to your energy through your connection to the Earth. I highly recommend using this technique before a challenging conversation, but you can also picture this while you are involved in the conversation. As with the Listening Bubble or the Energy Magnet, you can practice seeing yourself grounded in this way with your eyes open so that you can easily maintain that grounded and protected feeling the whole time.

If you want to take it a step further, you can add an affirmation of empowerment to your meditation.

Empowerment Affirmation

Affirmations are an excellent tool to help with so many different processes. An affirmation is a mental program, and here is how it works. If you have the same pattern of thought repeated over and over again, it becomes a significant neural pathway that your brain automatically uses without you having to think about it. It is the same way habits are formed, both good and bad, and can contribute to how you think, believe, and feel about the world.

52

CHAPTER 7
ENERGY SHIELDS/MASTERING
SOME PROTECTION

To avoid the effects of dark magic and other harmful energies, it is always wise to adopt some techniques that protect you. In this blog post, learn how to master some protection techniques that will help you beat any dark mage in their own game.

1. Energy Shields

Energy shields are a way of protecting yourself from unnecessary harm with the help of trusty chi energy. They can be drawn up around your body or yourself as a whole for protection from dark magic and any other hostile energy. To draw up an energy shield, go into a meditative state and take deep breaths as per usual. As you're taking deep breaths, inhale deeply while chanting "I am peaceful. I am peaceful. I am peaceful." Then, exhale while chanting "I am protective. I am protective. I am protective."

2. Energy Blasts

Energy blasts are a useful method of fighting past the effects of dark magic and any other harmful energies. To draw up an energy blast, go into a meditative state and take deep breaths as per usual. As you're taking deep breaths, inhale deeply while chanting "I release my energy blast from my body." Visualize your breath as a flame of fire or lightning coming out of your body and destroying all the dark magic in its path.

3. Negative or Positive Energy

Sometimes, your body is in a dangerous condition that can be either negative or positive. In this article, we are talking about your condition and not the surrounding area. To draw up negative energy or protection from other harmful energies, go into a meditative state and take deep breaths as per usual. As you're taking deep breaths, inhale deeply while chanting "I am breathing in peace and harmony." Visualize the negative vibes leaving your body through your mouth as you exhale heavily.

4. Practice Daily

Practicing any of these techniques daily will help you practice whatever it is that you intend to do for the rest of your life. Practice makes perfect and you will feel better after practicing these techniques.

5. Make a Shield Bracelet

Make a shield bracelet and wear it whenever you want or need protection. This will temporarily protect you from energy attacks or any other harmful energy.

CHAPTER 8
CONTROL THE ABSORBING
OF OTHER PEOPLE'S ENERGY

Most people rely on their will to control when absorbing other people's energy is appropriate and when it isn't, but that's not necessarily a reliable way to know what's okay.

Many of us use subtler "cues" that we could rely on body language, tonality, posture, and the like. These are all ways in which we indicate what we're capable of feeling in our organism at the present moment.

Different schools of thought around the world have different sets of standards for what is considered "appropriate:"

- In some places, watching a violent movie is not considered appropriate for children.

- Some places think it is appropriate for boys to fight with each other at school.

- Some think it is appropriate to shout at their loved ones when they are emotional.

- Some worry that men wear the same clothes after several months or years because they are concerned about homosexuality.

Think that all of these are just cultural differences and many of them are rooted in superstition. That's why we don't have to worry too much; what matters more is to focus on how we feel inside when we're exposed to these situations. Similar to what a middle-aged woman said in a country where the standards are strict.

A situation can be short-lived or last for years on end. But this doesn't matter too much. The point is that they invariably involve a certain amount of outside energy which you absorb into yourself and, consequently, influence your feelings and emotions.

The question is: How do you know whether or not it's appropriate to absorb other people's energy? You can use an instinctive approach and trust your feelings at the time, but I prefer a more scientific approach.

I think that all of us can find a set of universal standards to choose when it is appropriate and when it is not.

It's also clear that someone ill doesn't need to fight with a partner because he's not able to focus his attention and energy on the important things in life. Someone ill needs to focus his attention and energy on getting well again.

Finally, it's also clear that someone angry at another person doesn't need to say "I love you," because it won't make things better but will, indeed, make them worse.

There are other situations where all people can understand the appropriateness or inappropriateness of what they're doing because they can use the "how we feel inside" approach. It's clear to us that it's appropriate for children to be selfish because the outside world isn't full of useful energy, but energy that isn't harmful. Without a doubt, it's not appropriate for a drunken man to go home with a woman he doesn't know, as a lady who has been drinking isn't able to focus her attention and energy on the things that are important in life.

Someone who has experienced something violent doesn't need to laugh at someone else's being violent, because laughter is an expression of joy and gives energy.

All of these examples involving children and violence, a drunken man who goes home with a woman he doesn't know and someone angry at another person are examples where we can understand the appropriateness (or inappropriateness) of what we're doing by using our feelings inside at the time.

It's also clear that all children know how to tell if it's appropriate for them to absorb other people's energy or not because they know whether or not it feels good when they do it.

Indeed, most children naturally feel guilty when they learn about natural disasters that happen because they need to understand that the outside world is full of harmful energy which must be avoided whenever possible.

CHAPTER 9
MEDITATION

Meditation can be very difficult for some people, especially those who suffer from anxiety or some other mental health condition. For them, a guided meditation session might be a perfect way to deal with these situations and gain tranquility and mental peace.

Guided meditation sessions for empaths are as accessible as any other form of guided meditation online. They will allow your mind and body to heal along with the restorative power of our natural world at large, so there is no doubt in your ability to achieve peace in such an effortful time.

Best Ways to Do It Safely

1. Create a safe and clean space

Before you begin any self-guided meditation session, you must make sure that you've cleared your mind of all clutter and stress. There should be no other things disturbing your concentration, in that case, you must block them out. By doing this, your mind will remain clean so that we can all focus on relaxing.

It is quite likely that if you're an empath, then you have had experience with stress as an effect of having too many things in your life at the same time. You can take some time to create a space for this session to fit in, making it warm and cozy but not too distracting or cluttered.

2. Tune out the noise

Meditation is often used as a way of bringing clarity and mental peace, but it's very easy to ignore if you're listening to other distractions. People are good at spacing out when they have little else to think about than their inner world, so be sure to set aside some time where your mind won't be bothered by others yet still allowed to concentrate on the task at hand.

One way of doing this is by getting into a warm bath before your meditation session. That way, you will still be in the water while you meditate, which can be amazingly effective in your healing process.

3. Create a mantra

A mantra is a word or series of words that will help guide your mind into a relaxed and peaceful state. It is like having a lighthouse to help guide you back to safety when the night seems frightening and dark. By using this mantra, you're creating a sense of focus that will allow you to relax.

Some people like to use specially selected songs while they mediate or simple phrases that they want to hold on tight to throughout their session. It's up to you to make sure that the words themselves are soothing and relaxing before you choose them.

4. Breath exercise

It's easy to become distracted when you meditate and we cannot always tell when we're becoming so. Breathing exercises can be used as a way of controlling your mind and keeping it focused, but they can also help you relax even more after your session is over. When taking deep breaths at regular intervals during your meditation session, it will allow your body to feel relaxed and comfortable, which can lead to a deeper sense of inward peace within yourself.

5. Let go

It's important to let go of all stress and anxiety to relax. If you find yourself getting irritated or stressed out during your session, it may be time to take a break and think about what is making you feel so uncomfortable. Once you're able to sort out the problem, you can come back with a renewed sense of peace, as well as transformed energy.

6. Close your eyes

Some people prefer closing their eyes during meditation, though others feel more comfortable keeping them open. Closing your eyes will help your body become more relaxed and allow you to focus a bit more completely on the relaxation that you're achieving.

7. Allow your body to relax

If you're stressed out, there's always a worry in the back of your mind about something or someone causing us to be as such. Trying not to get too unsettled is vital to reach this state, especially when meditating. If you find yourself becoming anxious, just return your attention to your breath and relax into the moment as much as possible over again.

We are often told that our mind is what makes us who we are and if we can learn how to control it, we can achieve peace and tranquility within ourselves. Meditation can be a very easy way to achieve this, allowing you to focus and use your mind differently.

8. Listen to music

As mentioned above, music is another way that we can distract ourselves from stress and anxiety. When we listen to it, however, not only do we distract ourselves from the stress that we might otherwise be experiencing, but it also serves as a guide through meditation. You must listen to music in an environment where you're at ease so that you aren't distracted by external sounds or concerns.

9. Try a guided meditation

Guided meditation comes with a pre-recorded version from someone who has achieved this state before and can help you achieve it as well through their soothing words. These can be very beneficial for those who are looking for extra guidance in the form of a voice to follow and tips on how to relax the stress away.

10. Be relaxed

Many people believe that they're relaxed when they aren't, so you need to make sure that you're aware of this. When you're relaxed, you'll be able to allow your mind to be at peace and you won't have so much trouble with distractions and stress.

11. Use a timer

Many people find that the timer they use is very helpful in their meditation sessions because it will remind them when it's time to move on. This will be good for many reasons, one of which is that you might, otherwise, forget the time and complete your session before the allotted time is up. A timer can also help you control the time of day you meditate so that only when it's a decent time of day you choose to begin your session if needed.

12. Choose a specific time of day

Meditation is good for aiding in the healing process, especially if you're not feeling well. But it's best to do this at specific times during the day rather than whenever convenient. This will help you get into the proper frame of mind and allow your body to become more relaxed over time as you gain control of it while practicing meditation.

13. Be in an environment that feels comfortable

It's good to have a comfortable place where you can meditate, even if this means taking part in your session in your dorm room or at home. Make sure that you have a comfortable bed to sleep in, a nice desk to sit on, and a space to meditate.

14. Be relaxed

If you're not relaxed before your session begins, it will be difficult to experience the type of relief that is achieved during meditation, so strive to relax as much as possible beforehand. Sit down and take deep breaths until you feel an overwhelming sense of peace washing over your body while it's at rest. This will help guide your thoughts into a deeper area of calm and tranquility.

15. Enjoy the silence

You may hear things outside of you or around you while meditating and you're not supposed to worry about this as it is part of the process. However, if you hear distracting noises, it may be best to meditate in a quieter environment where there's no distraction. This way, your thoughts can remain within yourself rather than outside of your mind.

16. Sit in a lotus position

This is one of the more relaxing positions to sit during meditation, so try to find a comfortable position for you in which your lower leg is resting on top of the other leg. This will help maximize movement, as well as relaxation for your body and mind during meditation.

17. Avoid distractions

If you're going to meditate, you'll want to make sure that any distractions that are going on around you are minimized so that you can focus on your exercise. Your attention needs to be focused solely on the meditation because if it's not, it will most likely be followed by conflict or stress. You might also want to avoid socializing with others while meditating, to prevent yourself from being distracted and placed into an awkward situation.

18. Use a soothing song

Music is great to listen to while attempting to meditate because it can distract you from any other worries or concerns that might, otherwise, be consuming your thoughts. It's also great for helping to calm you down and make you feel relaxed so that your meditation session can be as successful as possible.

19. Listen to an audio recording

If you don't know any guided meditation techniques, then it may help to use an audio recording that comes with a voice telling you what to do while at the same time guiding your body into the proper position. This will help make sure that you're doing everything right so that your session can go off without a hitch and only take place in silence without distractions.

20. Meditate on thoughts of love

This is one sort of guided meditation that is very helpful to many people because it helps their body become relaxed and eased in a "healing" way. Meditating on thoughts of love will help your mind and body relax, making you feel more at peace with yourself, others, and the world.

21. Use a mantra that is helpful to you

Another great way to meditate is to use a mantra or phrase that you can say to yourself repeatedly while in your session. This will help you guide your mind into a deeper state of relaxation so that you can realize all of the benefits of meditation while also gaining control over your own body, as well as your mind.

22. Find your inner peace

Many people believe that meditation helps them to achieve peace, as well as harmony with their mind, body, and spirit. The ability to meditate comes in handy for many reasons but it's best done when you feel at your best and peaceful within yourself so that all of the benefits can be attained and maximized for your soul.

23. Become more aware

One of the most important aspects of meditation is helping a person become more aware of their surroundings so that they can use this new sense of awareness to their advantage after the session ends. This can be a rewarding experience for many people because it will help them in all areas of their life, especially at work and school, so be sure that you're aware of how to meditate properly when you attempt to do so.

24. Meditate with a visualization

You may not want to use an audio recording when it comes to meditating because you want to remain unguided throughout your session. In this case, you can use different visualization exercises during your practice time so that your mind will focus on something other than the things that are happening around you. This is very useful in some situations but not all, so it's best if you try it out and see if it's something that works for you or not.

25. Think about what you want

You may not know what you want to achieve during your meditation, but you can always choose to think about something that you'd like instead. This will help your mind's focus become clearer, especially when it's a goal that can be easily achieved and one that is worth being focused on during your session.

26. Think about your day

If you have a busy schedule, then this is the perfect time to think
about the things that happen and how they will affect your future and present life situations. This will assist you in becoming aware of everything going on in your life and how they all affect

each other so that you don't get too confused after meditating.

27. Meditate the right way

Meditation can be dependable when you have a plan for it, so try to find out the best way to meditate and then stick with it because there's no wrong way. There are times in which meditating may be best done at night or during certain times of the day but if this is not the best time for you, then it's okay to adapt your session according to what your body needs at that time. This will help ensure that you're receiving all of the benefits from meditation rather than just a few here and there.

28. Focus on what you're doing

You can use this as a way of becoming more aware of all of the tasks you need to complete and then make this a goal to work toward achieving before your session ends. This will help guide many people into doing their best work when they try to meditate, which is always a great thing.

29. Take your time

If you try, then you can always be at peace while you're meditating but it's best if you take your time. There are a few people who feel that they have to rush their session to achieve something, but this is a mistake many people make. Because meditation is so important, you shouldn't rush and it's never too late to change your mind about what you're doing or how long it should take. You should give yourself plenty of time so that you can ease into your session and take it as slowly as possible.

CHAPTER 10
SPIRITUAL AWAKENING

A summons to greater consciousness and mental awareness is referred to as spiritual awakening. Personal change and a modification in one's perspective occur because of a spiritual awakening. A transformation in one's conceptual framework occurs when one experiences a spiritual awakening.

Causes of Spiritual Awakening

Many individuals experience spiritual awakening because of life-changing incidents. For the others, the change is slow and subtle.

1. A traumatic event

The one has a significant and negative influence on our physiological and emotional health. It is usually followed by a protracted period of recovery. Struggling through one sort of maltreatment or experiencing a major accident are examples of traumatic experiences.

2. Life-altering experiences

These are the kinds of things, which have the power to alter the direction of life. A life-altering event might be a divorce, the loss of a close one, or even a terrible illness.

3. Existential crisis

Also referred to as Soul's Dark Night. A person experiencing an existential crisis begins to wonder about the meaning and goal of existence. It is frequently characterized by depression. This is not always the situation when a life-changing incident occurs.

4. Near-death Incident (NDE)

This is a self-explanatory statement. Many persons who have had a near-death experience have also mentioned coming into touch with entities from another side. As you might expect, such an event has a tremendous impact on one's view of life.

Natural Awakening

This is an uncontrollable waking process. It occurs after the completion of a practice that results in a change in conscious perception. Practices that may help you become more mindful include mindfulness, meditation, developing a strong emotional attachment to plants and animals, practice self-transformation.

Signs of Spiritual Awakening

1. A greater tendency for letting things unfold rather than forcing them.

2. Frequent bouts of smiling.

3. A sense of being linked to people and nature.

4. Overwhelming expressions of gratitude regularly.

5. The proclivity to think or behave impulsively rather than

out of dread based on previous experiences.

6. An undeniable capacity to cherish every moment.

7. An inability to be concerned.

8. A lack of enthusiasm for combat.

9. A lack of interest in analyzing other people's behavior.

10. A lack of desire to pass judgment on others.

11. A lack of desire to judge oneself.

12. Starting to love and expect nothing in return.

Spirit Guides

Spirit Guides are advanced spiritual beings entrusted to the soul to assist lead, heal, and educate you throughout this incarnation, similar to guardian angels. Once we consciously link to the Guides, they are completely done with their lifetimes and experiences on the Earthly level, and the guides have a greater perspective and a deeper understanding to impart. The majority of individuals communicate with their Guides via meditation. Setting a sincere intention that connects you with your guides is the most crucial thing you can do. After that, settle into a silent and relaxed state and concentrate on your breathing. Connecting to your guides may take the form of some of these — no need to set any particular expectations for yourself, as everyone's relationship is unique and genuine:

- A feeling of peace, relaxation, support, as well as love washing over you.

- Getting a random thought, recollection, or inspiration occurs to you.

- Sensing the power of a particular color in the environment or within yourself.

How do you get in touch with your spirit guides?

When seeking to interact with your spirit guides, the most crucial component is to establish your desire to interact and then trust whatever appears after that, even if it is not as wonderful as you had thought. Begin your meditation by saying loudly or in the head something like Thanks to your Spirit Guides for communicating with me. Maybe you are a transparent channel for a guide to provide you with thoughts, sentiments, and directions. Consider the signs while communicating with your spirit guides.

Inquire for signs

Your spirit guides are always there for you, even if you are not into meditation, offering you the messages of motivation, encouragement, and instruction. Choose a particular sign to represent confirmation from the spirit guides that means you are linked to them or even on the correct track. A beloved animal or a bird, your favorite song, repeated numerical sequences, or anything, which bears special importance to you, might be a signal with your guardians. You do not have to look for your Guide sign; instead, be willing to receive it in unexpected ways. If you chose a dolphin as a sign, it does not always manifest itself in the form of witnessing a real dolphin in the ocean. Pay attention when others near you mention dolphins, have seen an image of a dolphin on somebody's t-shirt, or just dolphins appear in the dreams. The last stage in this procedure is to express thankfulness and acknowledgment whenever you get a sign. Moreover, let your spirit guides know that you have heard their word and are pleased to be linked; just say thank you within your head or a tiny smile.

CHAPTER 11
THIRD EYE

P sychic empaths can feel what others are feeling. They can also, through practice and training, learn how to project this onto subjects and perform readings like a clairvoyant. This is because they've got the third eye — the psychic eye — which is connected to their sixth sense and intuition. It's believed that we all have a third eye but that some people just use it more than others. Some people can simply sense the emotions of others, some others can channel their intuition and some can do both.

A psychic empath can be defined as a person who can intuitively know how others are feeling and if they can't sense it on a conscious level, then they are likely to sense it on an unconscious level. They do not necessarily need to be psychics for this to happen. Psychic empaths help others with their powers, helping them gain strength through positive thinking and positive visualization, which takes us back to the whole law of attraction thing. Positive thinking can be defined as being positive in your thoughts and actions.

A psychic empath has strong empathy skills, that allow them to know exactly what someone is feeling and if they do not have that contact with the person then they are likely to sense it, for instance, by smelling the scent of someone else's perfume or seeing a ghostly figure out of the corner of their eye.

A psychic empath can also be a channeler. A channeler is someone who can talk to spirits, get information, and learn the truth about their life and death. The reason why this exists is that the psychic empath can get information by concentrating on what their sixth sense is detecting. They are an excellent judge of character, especially if they have had previous experiences with said person, or even if they have just got the impression that something has happened recently regarding that person.

Others are more intuitive than others. Some people innately can read the energy that surrounds us. They use it to interpret, analyze, and sometimes predict what will happen in the world around them. For example, they might feel something is going to happen that day or they may just come up with a gut feeling about what will happen somewhere in the country. They can usually get it right but they'll also feel what others are feeling.

Psychic empaths can also sense the feelings of others by touching an object that has been touched by another person or handled. They will feel the energy that has transferred to the object and they'll be able to interpret this. Some psychic empaths can get direct information from people especially if they are skilled in a type of clairvoyant reading. All this means that the psychic empath is so sensitive to the emotions of others that it can become overwhelming at times and cause them to feel down or stressed out. To avoid this, they need to understand emotions, heal themselves and learn how to shield themselves from the negativity of others.

To understand emotions, psychic empaths need to understand how emotions affect us. It's not enough to just know how other people feel — you need to know how you feel and why you feel it so that you can learn how to manage your own emotions. Emotions manifest themselves in different ways, in the way that we think, act, and the way that we communicate with others. Sometimes, they are subtle and occasionally they are very obvious.

Emotions can change form. They can be expressed in different ways and can sometimes come in many forms, including physical symptoms. It's not just one emotion, but many that together make up a person's personality. For example, when a parent meets a child with Down syndrome, they may feel love and happiness but it can also feel like an emotional rollercoaster and there are lots of emotions involved too. The same is true of children who have been neglected and abused.

76

CHAPTER 12
CHAKRAS

I n Sanskrit, the ancient Indian language that describes everything we are talking about, chakra translates to mean "wheel" or "disk." You could also see each as a swirling vortex. These wheels are the main energy centers of your body, or rather your "subtle-body," as it is often termed in yogic texts.

The colors, from the base to the head, form the colors of the rainbow. Each chakra also has qualities, similar to how you might describe human qualities. For example, the fourth chakra, (or heart chakra) lies where your heart is in your chest. If you were going to describe this chakra to someone, you might say that it is loving, open, generous, and warm. You might also say that it is overly protective, defensive, and afraid to give and receive love. When the heart chakra is balanced and open, the energy of this chakra allows for the generosity of love. If blocked or congested, the heart chakra can create closed energy, which prevents the flow of giving and receiving love and affection.

Since each chakra has its qualities, colors, and vibrations, they may seem to be individual, but one doesn't function well without the others also flowing. Sometimes, due to life experiences, physical or emotional trauma, diet, habits, and other factors, chakras can become imbalanced where they are either excessive (too much) or diminished (not enough). Additionally, a chakra can become blocked, which means there is a lack of flow, causing stagnation. These stagnations can, over time, lead to illness, disease, chronic health conditions, and mental health issues.

Along with its qualities, color, and vibrational quality, each chakra is also associated with specific organ systems in the body including glands, sex organs, digestive organs, body parts, etc.

The Base Chakra (Muladhara)

The base chakra is the beginning of the energetic journey in the subtle body. Its Sanskrit name means "root." It is the earth element. It is survival. It is the right "to have." It is here that the Kundalini energy is stored. This is the place of physical health, grounded Ness, stability, youthful quality, vitality, fight or flight instinct, and prosperity. It is connected to your sense of smell; the first sense you are aware of when you are born.

When your root chakra is imbalanced, you may experience feelings of insecurity, anger, disconnection, depression, shortage of patience, nervousness, greed, unnecessary fear, and lack. When this imbalance manifests in our physical bodies, it may appear as frequent illness, obesity, eating disorders, constipation, knee troubles, sciatica, and even hemorrhoids.

Since the root chakra is where the dormant Kundalini energy lives and rises from when awakened, it is important to recognize the qualities of the chakra and its connection to all the other chakras. However, one must not put all emphasis on this energy, and here is why: Kundalini's awakening begins here, but it may also end in the root chakra. Some experiences show that it can be the last chakra to truly awaken. The rest of the transformation through the chakras may occur first, but to achieve true balance, the energy of Kundalini must return to the beginning—to where the source of the energy awakening began.

The Second Chakra (Svadhisthana)

The second chakra is also often called the "sacral chakra." Its Sanskrit name means "sweetness." It is the water element. It is the place of emotion and sexuality. It is the right "to feel." This is the place of pleasure, fluid movement, creativity, and passion.

This chakra is associated with the color orange and is located in the area just below the navel in your lower abdomen and is associated with the bladder, female reproductive organs, lymphatic system, and pelvis. It is connected to the sense of taste. When your sacral chakra is balanced, you will feel happy, joyful, creative, passionate, and capable of connecting physically. This is also where the drive to procreate exists.

When your sacral chakra is imbalanced, you may feel unworthy, isolated, numb, stiff, overly sensitive, and emotional. You may also have a sexual addiction, otherwise, what is called sexual anorexia, hormone imbalance, and the potential for miscarriages or difficulty conceiving.

The Third Chakra (Manipura)

Its Sanskrit name means "lustrous gem." It is the fire element. It is power and energy. It is the right "to act." This is the place of personal power, the strength of will, and sense of purpose. The physical feature associated with the solar chakra is the adrenal glands. Your adrenal glands regulate metabolism, blood pressure, and your immune system.

When the chakra is in balance, you will feel the energy and drive, confidence, an active and cheerful disposition, and a strong sense of purpose. The opposite of balance would look like a deficiency of energy, a feeling of helplessness, weakness, timidity, and a submissive life approach.

The Fourth Chakra (Anahata)

This one is also known as the "heart chakra." The Sanskrit name for this chakra is translated as "unstruck," "unhurt," or "unbeaten." It is the air element. It is love and relationships. It is the right "to love;" this is the place of compassion and acceptance for the self and others, and a balance in all relationships. The physical component of this chakra is the thymus gland and lymph system, which help regulate immunity and fight disease and illness.

When the heart chakra is in balance, you will feel love, compassion, interconnectedness, and acceptance, life will flow smoothly, and there will be a general feeling of affection for everyone and everything—universal love. If the heart chakra is imbalanced, it can express this through excessiveness or deficiency. A deficient heart chakra can often look like low self-worth or low self-esteem, melancholy, isolation, depression, and inability to breathe deeply. Excessive heart chakra energy shows itself in the form of co-dependency, clingy behavior, and too much caretaking of others.

The Fifth Chakra (Vishuddhi)

The fifth chakra is also called the "throat chakra." The Sanskrit name for this chakra is translated as "purification." It is the element of ether or sound. It is communication. It is the right "to speak." This is the place of self-expression, speaking, soul song, and the ability to communicate with others. There are several physical features connected to this chakra, such as the already mentioned throat, jaw, neck, thyroid gland, teeth, ears, and esophagus; everything associated with speaking and listening.

When this chakra is balanced, you can enjoy clear and truthful self-expression, honest and good communication, creative expression, and affinity with yourself and others. There is also an ability to comprehend the balance of opposite forces with reverence, accepting the value of both light and dark, high and low, and that they each have a vital role in the harmony of all life energy.

The Sixth Chakra (Ajna)

The Sanskrit name for this chakra is translated as "perceive," or "to know." It is the light element. It is visual perception, intuition, and clairvoyance. It is the right "to see." This is the place of imagination, thought, telepathy, vision, and rational logic. The sixth chakra is associated with the color indigo and is situated between the eyes or behind the eyebrows. Its physical attribute is the pituitary and pineal gland. The pituitary gland regulates hormone secretions, while the pineal gland is involved in the regulation of sleep patterns and circadian rhythms.

When the sixth chakra is balanced, there are great abilities in perception, your mind is at ease and can process thoughts quickly, improve memory and intelligence, not afraid of death, you have a strong connection to your intuition, and can have clairvoyant and telepathic abilities.

The Seventh Chakra (Sahasrara)

The seventh chakra is also often called the "crown chakra." The Sanskrit name for this chakra is translated as "thousand-fold." It is the thought element. It is expanded consciousness. It is the right "to know." This is the place of understanding, of enlightenment. The crown chakra is associated with the color violet and is located at the top of the head, in the cerebral cortex. The physical component of this chakra includes the brain, hands, nervous system, and in parts the pituitary gland, creating a link to the sixth chakra.

When the seventh chakra is balanced, you will have an expanded consciousness that will lead to a transcendence of barriers projected by humanity, and the laws of nature have a greater understanding and acceptance of death, mortality, the immortality of the soul, increased and heightened spiritual gifts and capabilities, and the creation of miracles.

PART 2: PSYCHIC

CHAPTER 13
WHAT IS A PSYCHIC?

The scientific study of psychic, or psi (pronounced sigh), phenomena is known as "parapsychology." These are information exchanges between living things (mostly humans), between living things' brains and the environment (without the use of our regular senses), or direct effects of living things' minds on the environment (without the use of physical bodies or technology). Of course, these connections do not seem to be explained by recognized physical laws of nature at the moment, but that will not always be the case. Psi, by the way, is the word used by parapsychologists to describe these experiences since it is a simple phrase, indicating merely an unknown and being the twenty-third letter of the Greek alphabet.

To be psychic simply means that you have a method for gathering knowledge other than logical deduction or inference to solve issues. Whether we use jargon words like psi or ESP, whatever we're utilizing to get additional insight is something worth paying attention to; our brains are telling us, "There's a piece of information that needs to be considered, so consider it now!"

According to parapsychology's principles, everyone has some degree of psychic ability. Thus, those who proclaim themselves psychic may be from all walks of life. There are, however, some who refer to themselves as psychics with a capital P. "I am a Psychic," as opposed to "I am psychic," is a distinct expression. As a result, individuals who claim to be psychic have a greater understanding of their talents and, therefore, some control over them, according to their claims. Such a professional title (psychic, psychic reader, or psychic practitioner) typically implies that the individual doesn't have true control over their talents, but rather that they are aware of all the additional knowledge that enters their brains and may use or use it in various circumstances. Of course, there are many phonies out there—people who are not only not very psychic (nor are those who come to them as customers), but who are also conscious of their lack of psychic ability and falsely present themselves as "ones who know."

We must first define words before determining if certain individuals are more psychic than others. Psychics are those who have psychic talents and have had psychic experiences. Since the majority of people have had a psychic experience at some point in their life, and since parapsychology studies show that psi is equally distributed across the population, as are reports of psychic experiences, it seems that everyone is psychic to some degree. The issue of whether one individual is more psychic than another is a legitimate one, but one that is difficult to answer in each instance.

Psi is like musical ability, according to the comparison made to compare it to anything in science fiction. Whether you can tap your foot to a rhythm or perform a symphony on the piano, everyone possesses it to some degree. Recognizing and nurturing musical potential is crucial. Some individuals are musical prodigies, able to leap straight into the music with little or no instruction, while others, no matter how hard they try, will never be able to get beyond playing "Chopsticks." Psi is similar but not nearly as trainable. Knowing the difference between information received or seen via your regular senses and anything additional that comes through may be considered psychic. People who label themselves as psychics may filter out the noise that their senses take up and pick up fainter signals in the background.

Even though our society (particularly academics) argues otherwise and even mocks the idea, most individuals in the West think psychic contacts and experiences are at least conceivable, according to all surveys. According to a poll conducted by George Gallup Jr. and Jim Castelli in the late 1980s and published in the Los Angeles Times (Dick Roraback, "If There's a Ghost of a Chance, Americans Will Believe It," October 31, 1988), 46% of all Americans believe in extrasensory perception, 24% believe in the ability to receive information from the future (precognition), and 15% believe in the ability to see into the future (telepathy).

As a result, a sizable portion of the population believes in psychic encounters and has reported them. With such a large number of participants, opponents of parapsychology and many psychic practitioners frequently create the misleading impression that these encounters are abnormal. Psychic experiences, or those we refer to as psychic, are a natural component of the human experience. According to more recent surveys, college-educated individuals are more likely to believe in psi's actuality, or at least its possibility, with up to 7 out of 10 people believing in some kind of psychic experience. Millions of individuals have claimed to have had psychic or paranormal encounters. Parapsychologists investigate these events and attempt to figure out what could be causing them. We're also searching for physical explanations for how psi works, such as how individuals can receive knowledge from the future, the past, or thousands of kilometers distant, or how we can influence that computer across the room. We investigate how (psi) occurs, who (it affects), and why (it happens to those people).

Parapsychologists are those who examine people's subjective paranormal encounters (SPE). Dr. Vernon Neppe, neuropsychiatrist, and parapsychological researcher, created this term to explain what occurs to individuals. The SPE is a term that refers to any encounter that seems or feels paranormal or psychic. We term it subjective since the experience is out of the ordinary and may be classified as psychic because of our interpretation. This isn't to say that the SPE isn't about objective, actual events; it simply means that objective, genuine proof may not be accessible.

The interaction involving information streaming into someone's head is known as "Extrasensory Perception" (ESP). Psychokinetic (PK) is a word used by parapsychologists to describe physical interactions—the concept of mind over matter. It encompasses anything from psychic healing to influencing computers and other electronics to item movement. These manifestations occur naturally in people's lives. Therefore, parapsychologists research them both in and out of the laboratory. Parapsychologists investigate psychic experiences using the scientific method, which entails much more than just gathering tales from individuals. Furthermore, the concept that the human personality, spirit, soul, or mind may survive the death of the body has piqued the interest of parapsychologists from its inception and even has its subsection of psi phenomena known as "Survival of Bodily Death."

To go further into the categories, ESP is fundamentally open since our brains receive data from outside sources. We call it telepathy, or mind-to-mind communication when information seems to originate in the mind of another person (or even an animal). Unlike what you may see on TV, this does not imply that someone can read another person's thoughts. It's more about the concept of pictures, feelings, and information being immediately exchanged between 2 or more minds. In terms of dreams, we're looking at the notion that information from other people's brains or experiences makes its way into ours, sometimes leading to reciprocal or shared dreaming.

CHAPTER 14
WHAT ARE THE PSYCHIC
ABILITIES?

O ne thing that people who are perhaps more in touch with their intuition often wonder about when they get the feeling that something is going wrong is: am I just anxious and paranoid, or is my sense of foreboding legitimate? The trick that often works to get to the bottom of the doubt about your feeling and know if it's just anxiety or a real premonition is: if you feel a sudden flash of foreboding or some sense that something is going wrong and then it goes away, that's your intuition. Pay attention to that feeling and listen to what it's telling you, what it's warning you. It can be very important. However, it won't stay with you for long, so do your best to interpret it while it's there; you can even write down what you feel. If you have the feeling that something is wrong and you can't stop thinking about it all day long, to the point where you overthink it and overanalyze it to try to figure out what it means and how you can fix it, to the point where you are very upset and it won't get out of your head, it is more likely to be anxiety and not a true psychic prediction in this case. It's easy to tell when it's anxiety because the feeling won't leave you alone.

Using only your reserve of energy is usually not the best way to practice clairvoyance, as it is limited (unlike that of the universe, which is unlimited) and can/will run out very quickly. If you get a premonition out of the blue (e.g., receiving a premonition even though you were not intending to receive it), it will leave you no option to be helped by the energy of the universe — but if you set out to do a psychic reading, it is important not to use your limited supply of energy and attempt the reading and receive premonitions without help.

The more your psychic powers begin to show themselves, the higher your vibration will be. The higher your vibration and energy, the less time you will want to spend around negative people or doing negative things. Don't be surprised if, while you are on your psychic journey, your eyes open to the negativity and negative habits of some of the people in your life. This is a completely normal part of the psychic journey, and you may end up feeling the need to cut certain people out of your life or stop doing certain negative activities you used to participate in. Unnecessary drama, rudeness, gossip, harmful behavior, etc., are all examples of things that you will begin to have the strong urge to avoid or stop. This is not to say that you can't indulge in your favorite reality show once in a while, or cut a friend out of your life because they are struggling with an addiction or because they are having a rough day and are angry with you or negative in the sense that they are sad and perhaps struggle with depression. However, people who are constantly negative and want to drag others down with them are not someone you want to have around. If you feel it is the right thing and will ultimately bring you happiness and empower you on your journey, then it is best to move away from these people (as gently as possible, without being rude or mean about it, be polite and sensitive if you feel they owe it to you) or stop doing these things that bring negativity into your life. Negativity is extremely draining for non-psychics, so you can imagine what it does to someone who is probably going to be quite vulnerable to the emotions, thoughts, and energy of others. That's why psychics should avoid negativity.

Vivid dreams are a sure sign of this. You'll probably notice that the more in tune you are with yourself and your abilities, the more vivid your dreams will be. If you are someone who rarely dreams or rarely remembers your dreams (and if you do, they are only vague images and feelings), you will notice an increase in your dreams, and you will be able to remember them more vividly. This is because once your psychic powers are awakened, your subconscious is more liberated and less blocked, so dreams flow more naturally.

Along with vivid dreams and tingling sensations, you may also experience an increased frequency of headaches. If you do it, consult a doctor to be sure. It could be a sign that your mental abilities are straining and tiring from the psychic practice you've been doing. The amount of energy you have to use to connect to yourself and focus on your intuition and the psychic realm is great, and even if you connect to the energy of the universe, it can still be a great strain and tension on the brain of a beginning psychic. Fear not, though: the headaches should start to dissipate as you progress and develop your skills, as well as become stronger and more focused.

You may also notice your other senses sharpening now that you are on the path to psychic awareness. If you have noticed that you no longer need subtitles to turn on when watching a movie, your palette has changed slightly, your eyes seem sharper than usual, or colors become more vivid, you are more sensitive to certain tissues, and you can pick up and locate smells much more easily, this can be attributed to your increased psychic potential. After all, you are heightening your sixth sense; it is natural for others to heighten their capacity as well. Now, if you're frustrated that you still need your glasses even though your psychic abilities are increasing, just remember that becoming psychic isn't a cure-all. It's not going to allow you to suddenly see with 20/20 vision or give you a refined palette; it may just heighten your senses slightly, that's all. It's just a sign of increased power.

An increase or development of psychometry is also common for new psychics. Psychometry is when you can feel the energy or history related to an object just by touching it. Over time, you may even have premonitions associated with the object, but while you are a beginner, you may simply notice that you can feel the energy of a certain object, often not on purpose. This is quite common in antique stores. Rubbing an old silver mirror, locket, jewelry, or any kind of antique relic may give you a strange sense of longing for seemingly no reason, but this may be due to the history of the object or its owner. If you are moving soon and will be viewing an open house, to get an idea of whether the house is right for you, consider the energy of the place as well. Run your hands over the walls, counters, and furniture in each room. This should give you a good indication of whether or not there is an excess of negative energy or whether or not you/the person you are moving in with and the house will be a good fit energetically. You will often hear of people getting the creeps and feeling a sense of evil or negative energy upon entering a house and later discovering that the murder or some other horrible event took place at some point. This is because they pick up the energy of space through psychometry. People with more developed intuition and psychic abilities are more likely to pick up on energy, so if they start to perceive things like this when they touch them, it's a good sign that they are on the right track.

CHAPTER 15
HOW TO DEVELOP PSYCHIC ABILITIES?

Since we are all born with innate psychic abilities and they are just sleeping within us, awakening and developing your psychic abilities mean that you would be utilizing your full potential. You are making use of something already available to you. You just need to learn how to use it properly and how to live with it because having your psychic abilities unlocked is going to change you. So, if you do not know how to deal with your awakened psychic abilities it is going to be hard and you will feel more pain and suffering. You are going to be filled with negative energies and it might cause you to mentally explode.

On the other hand, learning to develop and use your abilities properly is going to help you in many ways. You will be able to learn more about yourself and you will understand your feelings and emotions even further. You will be able to know what your goals truly are and your psychic abilities will be able to help you achieve them. It can also help guide you on how to deal with certain conflicts that may come your way. Being a psychic can also tell you which people or situations you should avoid. If a person or place is filled with negative energies, it is a good idea to stay away from that person or place.

Your creative energy will also grow. Also, your life will have a higher positivity overall. You will be happier and you will be able to spread happiness to everyone around you.

Being a psychic will not only allow you to help yourself, but it will also allow you to help other people. If one of your friends or family members is having trouble with their feelings and emotions, you can help them understand themselves and try to figure out what is causing those negative feelings and emotions. Once you learn about the root of their negative emotions, both can brainstorm ideas on how you are going to deal with it. Learning to let go is a good practice especially if you do not have any more options and cannot control the situation. Your psychic abilities can also help you guide people who have lost their way. If they are confused and do not know what to do next, you can support them and find out what is truly going to make them happy. Being filled with positive energy is not the only thing that a psychic can do, they can also spread the positive energy to other people to help the world be a better place for everyone.

Ways to Develop Your Psychic Abilities

There are 2 types of people in this world, the talent types, and the effort types. Some people have a talent for dancing or singing and they can be good at it with minimal effort. Meanwhile, other people need to exert more effort for them to be on the same level as the ones who are talented. This is also the same for psychics, some of us can develop our psychic abilities in a short time. However, for others, it can be a long and difficult journey. Some of us can even unlock our psychic abilities without any help from someone who knows how to unlock it. They can unlock their psychic abilities on their own. Not all of us are talented, most people are the effort types but most success comes from effort.

1. Understand yourself

The first thing you need to do on your way to developing your psychic abilities is to know more about yourself. You need to understand what you want to do and what makes you truly happy. Once you can understand yourself, you will be able to trust yourself even more. It is like how we are more likely to trust someone that we know rather than someone that we do not know. Understand yourself, trust yourself, and believe in yourself. You can achieve anything as long as you put your mind to it and you persevere. Believe in yourself and after a long time all that small progress will accumulate and you will see how far you have come and how much you have achieved. Every one of us has innate psychic abilities that are sleeping inside of us.

2. Find a place you can relax

It is the same with any other activity, if you are distracted you will not be able to do what you are doing correctly. If you are studying for a test in a noisy environment, you will not learn anything and will most likely fail your upcoming exam. You can choose your room if it is quiet and you are alone. You can also choose a park that does not have a lot of people and there are no noises from passing cars or other vehicles. If you are near a beach or a forest, that could also be a great place to choose since being in nature is beneficial to us psychics because of the positive energy that is coming from nature.

3. Meditation

It produces a calm and tranquil state of mind that will allow us to be more focused which will make us more self-aware. While meditating, our awareness of our surroundings will also increase and we will be able to feel and sense the presence of the energies that are around us. While we are in a deep state of relaxation because of meditation, it will help us manage our stress in life and reduce the negative effects of the negative energies that we absorb. Connecting with your spirit guides is also best done while you are meditating.

Before you start your meditation, you should first go to the place that you have chosen where it is comfortable and you can relax. It is also recommended that the place is quiet, if the place has noises, make sure that they will not distract you from meditating. After that, find a comfortable position where you can concentrate and relax, you can either sit or stand depending on what will make you more relaxed and comfortable. If you are too relaxed, it can make you lose focus and if you are too focused, it might make you stiff and you will not be able to relax so you need to find the right spot that is right for you because not everyone is the same and they can be relaxed at a different state. While your eyes are closed, take a long deep breath and start to visualize an object that you like or a place where you want to be. You can also start to communicate with your spirit guide by asking them to send you a visual message or try talking to them then make sure to listen carefully and for them to respond. You can also try to feel and sense the energies that are around you. If you are meditating outside and there are other people around you, you can try to pick a certain someone and try to sense the energy they are releasing. And based on their energy, try to sense what emotion they are currently feeling. Make sure you are not relying on visual cues and just use your mind to sense their emotions. Do not just assume they are sad because you saw them looking sad, try to concentrate and be more specific with their emotions. They may be disappointed or they may be feeling lost and not just simply sad.

4. Visualization practice

Visualization practice is an exercise that will help you develop the power of your mind to see things clearer. First, you need to choose an object and place it in front of you. Focus on the object you chose and look at it very carefully. You can use a flower, a fruit, or even a simple pen. Take a good look at the object and try to remember as much detail as you can. Try to focus on the shape, color, length, width, height, how it feels, how much it weighs, and all the other things you can associate with that object. After taking a very good look at your object, you then have to close your eyes and focus. Try to think about the object that is in front of you while you are keeping your eyes closed. Visualize the object in your mind as clearly as you can and with as many details as you possibly can. Imagine how the object feels when you touch it and how much it weighs when you pick it up. Think about the color of the object and its shape. After you picture the object, take a deep breath and open your eyes slowly. Check whether the details of the object in your mind are the same as the object in front of you. Repeat this exercise and try to get the image in your mind to be as close as possible to the original object that is in front of you. The image might be a bit blurry and not specific at first but after some time and if you continue practicing, you will be able to visualize the object perfectly and you can try to move on with a different object that is more complicated later on. This will help you have a more specific and clearer vision that is very detailed. This will also help you communicate with your spirit guide more effectively because the messages sent to your mind will be clearer. I recommend you to repeat this exercise a few times per week but make sure that you do not overdo it.

5. Give yourself time to rest

Resting is very important when you are developing your psychic abilities because you need the energy to perform psychic exercises. You would not be able to focus and remain calm and relaxed if you are tired. When we think of rest, the first thing that comes to our mind is lying down and taking a nap or sitting down and trying to relax but there are different types of resting for different kinds of tiredness. Physical rest is for when you are physically tired and your physical body needs to rest, mental rest is for when you are mentally tired and your mind needs a break from thinking; the emotional rest is for when you are emotionally tired and you need to rest your emotions; the social rest is for when you are socially tired and you need to take a break from socializing, and the creative rest is for when you are creatively stumped and you feel like you cannot come up with something creative which means that you need to take a break from creating.

Physical rest is needed when your physical body is tired. It is when your muscles and joints are aching, you need to take a nap or a long sleep to recover your strength. Mental rest, on the other hand, is about resting your mind. When you feel like
you are overthinking about every little detail in your life, you will feel tired. This is when you need to rest your mind and stop thinking for a bit. Take a step back and figure out what matters

and focus on those things instead of worrying about the things that are irrelevant or have little impact on your life.

Emotional rest is for when you feel emotionally tired and you need to rest your emotions. Do you ever wonder why you feel tired and drained when you are feeling sad and depressed after hearing bad news about something that you care about? Like when you get fired from work or your business proposal is turned down by a company. Being emotionally tired can leave you with a lack of motivation in continuing what you are doing or even make you unable to get up from bed because of the sadness that you are feeling. You can get an emotional rest by unloading all of the emotional things that you are feeling by talking to someone who is going to be willing to listen to you and not judge you. You can also write those feelings down on a piece of paper and burn that paper afterward. If you feel like you need professional help, do not hesitate to schedule a visit for a regular therapy session with a therapist that you trust. When you share your negative feelings with a friend or your therapist, you are going to feel lighter and better afterward. You will be able to gain back the motivation that you have lost and you will achieve your goals as long as you continue working toward them.

Social rest is something that a psychic will almost always need because they are sensitive to being around other people. Since psychics can get tired easily from socializing and meeting other people because of their ability to sense and feel other people's feelings and emotions, they would need to take a social rest every so often. Taking a break from socializing and meeting other people is required to gain back your energy. Spending alone time with yourself is a good idea so that you will not feel socially tired. Taking a long walk on the beach at night or meditating in your room will help you regain your social energy.

Creative rest is needed when you feel like you are stumped and you cannot think of a creative idea. You probably would not notice it often but after you have spent quite some time working on something creative like brainstorming for a theme of a birthday party that you are planning or thinking of a new design for your house that you want to renovate, you will feel tired and you would need a creative rest. Giving yourself a small break from all the creative thinking that you are doing and going to a place that can give you inspiration like going to a calm forest and camping for a couple of days or having a nice quiet time while reading a good book at home can help you replenish the creative resources that you have used up and will take the pressure of creating off of your mind.

CHAPTER 16
WHAT IS TAROT READING?

Tarot cards have been used for centuries by fortunetellers and spiritualists to read the future. In particular, they are seen as a way to look into the wisdom of our past, present, and future. Tarot reading is a form of divination in which the reader draws a set number of cards from what is usually called a "tarot" or "pip" deck — most often 78 cards in 13 suits — but could also be 22 cards in 4 suits, or variations thereof.

Helps us more fully understand ourselves and our lives through symbols that provide explanations for moments in our life that we have not yet been able to understand and process. Through these symbols, as well as drawing from a numerological system, an oracle, and a philosophy, we can access the deeper levels of our unconscious mind to understand and be guided through our life experiences. A tarot reading can help us reach a place of greater understanding and insight into ourselves, as well as others.

Originally used for fortune-telling in France around the 15th century by the Italian school of cartomancy, which is considered to be stable and safer than other methods. The subjects dealt with in these readings include love and money matters, but also spiritual matters, such as decisions about religion or beliefs.

Throughout history, the cards have been used in many different ways to help us gain insight into a variety of topics. Today they are used by people who take part in a variety of different groups and groups which are not religious or spiritual.

Tarot reading enables people to have an energetic connection with past and future events, allowing them to access their intuition and make decisions based on their intuition instead of relying on what they perceive is "right" or "wrong." Businesses that do tarot readings may use this energy during important decision-making processes.

Historically, tarot cards have been used by fortune tellers and spiritualists who believe that the cards can help them make sense of the universe. These practitioners generally use the cards to help people gain a deeper understanding of events or issues in their lives, as well as to see what the future could hold for them. The place where this takes place is called "cartomancy" ("Cartomania" in Greek). The origins of card reading range from ancient Egypt where it has been used for thousands of years, to China, which still uses it today with spiritual and psychological effects.

The most commonly used for card reading, have different meanings depending on the shapes and symbols on the cards themselves. The meanings of each card vary according to what type of deck it is, as well as by looking at the artwork on each card.

Widely used decks today are made up of 78 cards in total and consist of 4 suits: cups, swords, wands, and pentacles. However, many Tarot decks consist of far less or even more than this. For example, the Qabala Tarot is a deck of 78 cards, whereas the Thoth Tarot is a deck of 22 cards.

A tarot reading can be based upon the symbols used in one's Tarot deck or another type of reading system, such as an elemental reading. Elemental readings are just as ancient as tarot and are often used in conjunction with tarot to exchange information from both systems when in use. The most popular are: chakras (energy centers of the human body), crystals, runes or I Ching, or The Book of Changes. Virgin decks are also starting to appear and feature mythological representations rather than standardized images.

In the past, tarot card readings were done with a deck of 52 playing cards. These were associated with the 4 suits of spades, clubs, hearts, and diamonds. In today's world, these are sometimes called 'pips' where pips are not related to playing cards but rather represent 'past present, and future'. These decks consist of fairly generic images and lack the rich imagery associated with the actual Tarot decks found in traditional shops today.

Tarot decks consist of 78 cards, divided into 4 suits. The suits are cups, wands, swords, and pentacles. These images of these cards are said to be representative of the different stages of human lives.

The main difference between an actual tarot deck and the playing card deck is that the images on tarot cards are a collection of people, animals, and objects in medieval costumes which are supposed to be representative of different aspects of our life. The 22 remaining cards (those not part of a suit) are called "Major

Arcana." These images deal with more complex aspects, such as spirituality, or deeper experiences, such as love and hate.

CHAPTER 17
WHAT IS TEA LEAF
READING?

T ea leaf reading is a divination method by which tea leaves in the bottom of the cup are examined, either by the drinker or an outside reader, to predict information about one's future. It is also called tasseography.

A book published in Boston in 1888, entitled 'Tea Leaf Reading and Fortune Telling', describes the practice. It states that a person making tea should take care not to disturb the leaves at the bottom of the cup. In this way, future events will remain undisturbed and clear. The book notes that if a leaf is not easily identifiable, it may be a sign of coming news or other happenings about which it would be prudent to be prepared. It also gives instructions on how to read various types of tea leaves, including black, green, oolong, and herb teas from many countries.

Another early publication giving instructions on reading tea leaves was written by Franz Harary. In his book, 'Tea Fortune Telling,' he says to hold the cup in your hands and look at it from all sides. The way it looks can give you a clue about your present circumstances.

Harary begins with the premise that the tea leaves at bottom of the cup are already brewed and that you must use your intuition to discover their meaning. Because there will be very many different signs in a cup, the reader must first "clear" the cup of other signs, so as not to confuse these signals with those that come directly from spiritual sources. Clearing, according to Harary, consists of concentrating on expanding one's consciousness until it encompasses all things and one is aware of all knowledge. Harary states that by doing this a possibility of seeing the future will open up.

"With nothing in your hands and a cup set properly, you may see clearly what is the situation of your life at this moment. And once you see the future, you will be ready for it."

Harary goes on to state that if one illuminates all the signs with light from his consciousness, he will see his destiny. This is not only possible through tea leaf reading, but also through gazing at a crystal ball or other similar devices.

This is a broader term than fortune-telling, it usually involves predicting the future. Divination can involve prophecy and other forms of direct or indirect communication with the metaphysical. It can also include a means of obtaining answers to questions, using techniques, such as mediumship, psychography, and scrying.

Tea leaf reading may be classified as a branch of 'scrying', which involves gazing at natural objects until visions appear. According to Charles Leland's book 'The Gypsies', published in 1891, they claim that by the use of these media they can look into the unseen worlds, see the future, read one's thoughts, and reveal past events.

CHAPTER 18
WHAT IS AURA READING?

What is an aura, exactly? The energy field surrounding people gives you a sense of how they're as individuals. Auras are colored lights that emanate from people or energy that may be detected without touching them and can provide information about their personalities. Reading auras is difficult and takes a lot of work to perfect.

What Is an Aura?

All living creatures have an aura, which is an unseen exhalation or energetic field that encompasses them. Even a rock or a kitchen counter has an aura since everything has an electromagnet around it. Although the aura surrounds the whole body, it is also a part of every cell and reflects all life's delicate forces. As a result, rather than being something surrounding the body, it might be thought of as an extension.

The Greek word Avra, which means wind, inspired the term aura. Our personalities, lifestyles, ideas, and emotions are reflected in the energy that flows through our auras.

Our auras clearly show our emotional, bodily, and spiritual well-being. Some argue that the aura is nothing more than an electromagnetic phenomenon that should be disregarded. Others say it contains the glimmer of hope and houses our higher awareness, which gives us the energy we need to live and operate. Others believe that the aura is a mirror of ourselves and contains a comprehensive record of our history, current, and even tomorrow. In reality, it's most likely a mix of all of them.

While it is challenging to perceive aura colors without training, most individuals can readily feel the auras of others. Picking up on someone's "vibe" is a common name for this, and it's an apt one, given that the aura is an energy vibration. You've undoubtedly observed yourself pulled to the warm and welcoming energy of someone who exudes a pleasant vibration and repulses by the depressing energy of someone who exudes an unhappy vibration at some time.

The contrasted auras would look differently when observed visually because of the electromagnetic frequency at which they are resonating. Aura readings use the colors of the aura's energy to provide information about a people's emotional, intellectual, physiological, and spiritual well-being.

Aura and Science

Color exists in the aura, and the color is formed by light. When Sir Isaac Newton witnessed sunlight traveling through a glass prism and forming a rainbow in 1666, he was the first to show this. This was a game-changing revelation since everyone had previously assumed that color was an intrinsic element of
112 everything. Newton, like many individuals ahead of the pack, was mocked for his ideas.

However, he continued his investigations and saw what occurred when the light was transmitted between 2 prisms. The light from the first prism split into a rainbow, but after crossing through the secondary prism, the rainbow changed back into plain light. It successfully refuted his adversaries' claims that the color was already there within the glass prism and that sunlight merely picked up on it.

Refraction was discovered by Sir Isaac Newton. As light travels through the prism, it is refracted or "bent." Because red has the longest wavelength, it is refracted more diminutive than the other hues. Violet has a smaller wavelength and is the most refracted of all the colors.

When Goethe said, "Colors are the sorrows of light," he captured this well. He meant that once the white light's vibratory rhythm is reduced, the diverse hues become apparent. Some colors are absorbed when light strikes the surface of an item. The only colors we can see are those that are reflected in us. As a result, we see a green leaf as green because it has accumulated all of the other hues.

Darker colors absorb lighter than brighter colors. This is why, in the summer, we prefer to wear brighter colors.

Although light does not form auras, it is required to view them. While exposed to sunshine, auras are developed and expanded, and when they are inside, they shrink. In utter darkness, they shrink considerably more. However, they do not vanish and may be seen as tiny, thin blue energy lines.

7 Layers of Aura

Each human being is encompassed by an aura, which is an electromagnetic radiation discipline. If you look into the religious world, you'll see that this layer is incredibly colorful and has numerous levels around the body. These ranges are significant to all beings because they encapsulate the many parts of each soul and self. Humans are not the only living things that have these auras. Healers also see them among animals, lumber, and crops in the wild. Anything alive and breathing has an assertive discipline that others can observe.

This area may be broader or narrow depending on one's mood, well-being, and current behaviors. According to specific experts, this discipline encapsulates light enveloping and safeguarding your body from top to bottom.

Spiritual counselors believe that the gentle is thinner toward the bottom and grander toward the head. When you're with other people, the power you radiate with your body may either calm them down or make them worried, and this can all happen without you saying anything. They're arguing that negativity is all around them. There is, however, an assertive discipline whose vibrations may be felt by someone else, and it does not need a religious sensibility to recognize it.

Following are the 7 layers of an aura:

1. The etheric layer.

2. The emotional layer.

3. The mental layer.

4. The astral bridge layers.

5. The etheric template layers.

6. The celestial layer.

7. The causal layer.

1. Etheric layer

Your etheric power layer is the one nearest to your physical body. It's around 2 inches away from your skin and is also known as the "Nadis." It helps you regulate your physical awareness and has an intense radiation threshold in your power discipline.

Your organs, glands, physical stresses, and even your bones are considered to be covered with this coating of force. It has a blue-grey color and vibrates at around 15-20 cycles per minute, according to the manufacturer. Sedentary people may have a lesser etheric layer, while those who are more active may have a deeper one.

2. Emotional layer

The second layer is the nearest to the body and is responsible primarily for reflecting your emotions and sensations. It has a brilliant coloring wheel that spans all of the rainbow's colors and is related to the sacral chakra. Spiritualists may observe that this layer is hazy while you're under emotional distress. Because your emotions cause this layer to vary, it may be a method in the morning and another one at night. It can enter the etheric plane, allowing the emotional self to engage with the physical self.

3. Mental layer

The third aura, which is the psychic body, is located just outside the second layer. It's known as the "solar plexus chakra" since it houses both your mental and emotional functions. The human aura extends 3-8 inches beyond the physical body.

This layer is a brilliant yellow color, and it represents your psychological well-being. Thus, it should have a higher level of vibrations than the prior 2. The vibrations from this degree, which are closest to your shoulders, neck, and head, may be seen by others. This layer will be brighter if you're a strong individual who tends to have excessive thoughts.

However, if you have a negative psychological state and suffer from symptoms, such as depression or anxiety, it's understandable that your color may be subdued and less vibrant. Thankfully, by engaging in reading, meditation, or energy stimulating activities, you may produce this layer more colorful.

4. Astral bridge layer

A heavenly bridge is the fourth tier. This is because it links the higher vibration ranges with the lower vibration ranges in the third layer. It's a link that connects your power discipline to the next level of the human aura. In terms of coloring, you'll see all of the spectrum colors right here, but a healthy fourth section will be a beautiful pink shade.

The cardiovascular chakra is intimately linked to this location, and it is critical to your spiritual development. This region is around 8-12 inches out from your body and is one of the most chaotic. The insanity is caused by the movement of lower-range vibrations to the astral plane or higher vibrational fields.

This region will be strengthened by your love and excellent connections, while any disagreements in relationships will diminish. Some people regard this as a portal through which they may produce objectives and out-of-body experiences. Those who have attained religious enlightenment or want to expand their perspective should use this bridge area to connect to higher levels.

5. Etheric template layer

This layer is also known as the "human aura's etheric double physique." It's the fifth layer, and it corresponds to the fifth chakra directly. This layer has a higher vibration frequency and is around 1-2 feet away from your body. Some believe that your aura represents your physical existence in the spiritual world and that the colors will vary greatly.

Issues like your reputation, identity, and complete power are all included inside this portion of your aura. It may also help your body recover from sickness and keep track of pollutants entering your system. This region may also benefit from the use of healing sounds.

6. Celestial layer

Everyone speaks about the third eye chakra, which is the sixth layer of your aura. You may establish religious connections and bring internal light into your being here. This aura is around 2.5 feet out from the body, and it is here that you get assistance with your knowledge.

This region allows your religious and physical ideas to mix, and meditation aids in this process. This place possesses powerful and resonant vibrations that link to the heavenly realm. In addition to being empowered by love and light, you may get communication from angels and holy people.

7. Causal layer

The etheric template, the seventh layer, is all about your holy self. This aura extends approximately 3-5 feet from your body and has a very high frequency. The root chakra, also known as the "seventh chakra," is where the soul and ideas communicate.

This layer has a unique responsibility in that it is responsible for keeping all of your layers together. Hence it has a broader bandwidth than the others. This region has a vibrant golden or white tone, which represents spirit. This aura allows you to connect to your originator, and it is here that your religious growth takes place.

Although everyone has a religious affiliation, not everyone is willing to give up and open this territory. On the other hand, those who surrender might get more access to the almighty and improve their physical abilities.

Understanding Aura Layers

The human aura is divided into 7 levels, each of which is paradoxically positioned inside another. These auras are dictated and influenced by a person's physiological, mental, and emotional well-being. From the inside out, each of these layers radiates.

The first layer is the one that is nearest to your body, and the final layer, or the seventh, is the one that is furthest away from your existence. Surprisingly, there are 7 chakras, each of which is linked to the layers of your aura.

Each of these levels is responsible for data transmission via your force fields or chakras. Every layer's particular vibration increases in intensity as it travels inside on the outside. The vibrations are most potent in the layers closest to the outside.

Your physical health might have an impact on your aura. For instance, if you're in excellent health and have an overall positive feeling of well-being, your power concentration will be massive and spectacular. In reality, it may be many feet long.

However, if you're unwell, agitated, or exhausted, your mental discipline and vibrations will be compromised. Each layer is flowing or structural, and they help provide harmony to your human aura.

Aura Reading

Psychics and alternative medicine practitioners have been doing aura readings for many years. Aura reading may disclose a lot of information about a person. A skilled psychic with this extraordinary talent may frequently catch glimpses of a person's past, present, and future by observing the aura or spirit field.

Many elements about a person's life may be communicated adequately via the energy that envelopes their body. **Among them are the following:**

- Physical well-being.

- Disease.

- Emotional problems.

- Past.

It is possible to identify physical health disorders by scanning a person's energy field. Are they sluggish, or do they have problems with blocked arteries, high blood pressure, biogenesis, traumatic injuries like sprains and broken bones, or anything else? A psychic can see into a person's physical health by looking at their aura.

Furthermore, if a psychic issue has already occurred to the body, a psychic may detect this in an aura reading. As an outcome, even if the body is mended, the aura will have a crack in it, indicating precisely what occurred.

As a result, reading a person's aura may also be used to diagnose sickness and disease. That is why receiving an aura reading may be so beneficial. A qualified psychic may discover any internal illnesses you aren't aware of via an aura reading.

Aura readings may also provide information about mental well-being concerns. In a reading of your magnetic waves, a psychic will be able to tell whether you're suffering from anxiety, depression, or any other symptoms.

For both the viewer and the individual being read, an aura analysis is a very personal experience. Nothing can be kept hidden from you. They may be able to deceive you with their lies, but the truth will be exposed in their auras. Many individuals feel compelled to lie to boost their self-esteem.

Meaning of Aura Color

The 7 key chakras are represented by the colors of your aura: root, sacrum, solar thorax, heart, larynx, parietal eye, and crown. Your aura is made up of the above-mentioned auric layers and is related to these chakras. Knowing which colors

belong to particular chakras might aid in deciphering what your aura is trying to tell you.

Colors Are Important

When completing an aura reading, the colors of a person's aura are highly essential. We are born with an energy body, as you may know. Some cells produce vibrational frequencies inside that energy field.

Each has a unique energy field reflected in the acoustic wave of our auras' frequencies. Furthermore, most of us have a unique colored aura that may provide information about what is going on in our bodies and minds to an aura reader.

Of course, disease, stress, and other factors may alter the hues of our auras. Different hues denote different concepts. **Following, we'll go through some significant colors to pay attention to:**

Red

Potential: Entrepreneurial.

This is solid color for use. It instills in the individual a strong sense of self-worth and a drive to succeed. In childhood, this hue is frequently muted, especially if the individual is compelled to conform to the family's wishes. As a result, the aura might look squished and drab at times. The aura increases after a person achieve maturity. They can balance on their tiptoes, indicating that the individual is now capable of performing whatever it is that they are doing. People with a red foundation color usually acquire leadership roles because they have the requisite drive, enthusiasm, and charm to inspire others. They are also warm-hearted and loving. Red may also represent physical bravery. Nervousness and self-centeredness are red's bad characteristics.

Orange

Potential: Harmony and collaboration are the potentials of the color orange.

Orange is a warm, nurturing hue that you'll see as the background color in individuals that are inherently wise, discreet, and easygoing. They can put others at ease, and they often find themselves in situations where they must calm "turbulent seas." They are sensible, grounded, competent, and practical individuals who keep their feet firmly on the ground. Laziness and a "couldn't care less" attitude are 2 negative characteristics of orange.

Yellow

Potential: Yellow possibilities include creativity and mental brilliance.

Yellow-skinned people are passionate, impulsive, and changeable. They are sharp minds who like entertaining others as much as being amused. They are gregarious, social, and love engaging in extensive discussions about practically any subject. They are eager to learn, yet they often dabble and skim the surface of numerous areas rather than delving deeply into one. Yellow has 2 bad characteristics: shyness and a desire to lie.

Green

Potential: Restorative.

Green is a calming hue, and those who have it as their background are naturally serene and healing. They are helpful, dependable, and giving. They may look calm and laid-back, but when the situation calls for it, they may be abrasive and unyielding. The only way to persuade individuals with a green background to alter their beliefs is to convince them that the concept is their own. Green's negative characteristics include rigidity and a fixed attitude.

Blue

Potential: Blue has the potential for a wide range of uses.

Because these folks are inherently happy and energetic, blue is an excellent color to use as the base color. As a result, their auras are usually vast and vivid. They go through the same fluctuations as anybody else, yet they always seem to climb out of the ruts easily. People that have a blue background are always youthful at heart. They are genuine, truthful, and frequently communicate precisely what they are thinking. The difficulty in completing activities is a negative attribute of blue. They are typically better at getting things started, frequently with zeal than at finishing them.

Indigo

Potential: Indigo's potential is to take up responsibilities for others.

It may be difficult to distinguish this hue as the ground color since it can seem practically purple at times. Because it is a warm, comforting, and caring hue, those with it as their base color are more likely to work in a humanitarian capacity. They like assisting and supporting others, and they are happiest when they are among the people they care about.

The reluctance to say "No" is one of the indigo's flaws. Others may readily take advantage of these individuals.

Violet

Potential: Spiritual and intellectual growth are both possible with this color.

Bishops do not wear purple robes by accident. Violet is the base color for those who progress spiritually throughout their life. The intensity of this hue in their auras may tell you how far they've progressed. Many individuals with a violet background strive to hide this aspect of their personality.

This does not provide satisfaction, and they will realize that they are not living their life to their full potential. Their auras begin to develop and become more colorful as they study and bloom in knowledge and wisdom. Violet's bad feature is a superiority complex that may be off-putting to everyone else.

Silver

Potential: This is the idealism's color and its potential involves wonderful ideas.

Silver is seldom seen as the ground color in auras, while it is regularly seen as one of the other hues. People who choose it as their background color are full of brilliant ideas, but unfortunately, most of them are unworkable. These individuals are often demotivated and become dreamers rather than doers. Their advancement may delight to see if they get motivated and discover a worthwhile concept to pursue.

Gold

Potential: Gold's potential is limitless.

This is the most potent of all the colors to use as a ground color. It enables individuals to tackle large-scale undertakings and accomplish practically everything they put their minds to. They are individuals who are charming, hardworking, patient, and goal-oriented. They usually reach their pinnacle of accomplishment later in life. It's no surprise that the halos surrounding saints and other spiritual figures are frequently painted in gold, symbolizing their limitless potential.

Pink

Potential: Pink possibilities are material and financial prosperity.

The foundation color of determined, obstinate individuals is often this delicate-looking tint. They create lofty objectives for themselves and then pursue them with steadfast dedication. They are often found in supervisory roles and responsibilities, which is unsurprising. They are, nevertheless, humble and unpretentious folks who live a peaceful existence. They are also kind, compassionate, and kind and are happiest when surrounded by those they care about.

Bronze

Potential: Humanitarianism's bronze potential.

This hue is frequently associated with autumn and has an almost rusty aspect that may be very appealing. Bronze-colored people are kind, sympathetic, and charitable humanitarians. They have a kind and giving nature. As a result, kids often need to practice saying "no" since others are regularly forced to do so.

White

Potential: Enlightenment and insight.

White is a color of purity that is seldom used as a background color. White is just another term for light since it is the source of all colors. Self-effacing, meek, saintly humanitarians are those who have it. They usually look to be devoid of ego and appear to be more concerned about the well-being of others than their own. These individuals are often wise, as well as intelligent beyond their years.

How to Read/See Aura?

Developing auric sight

The aura's vibrations are quite feeble; otherwise, you should be able to view the aura even without effort. **To view the aura through your own eyes, you must first figure out how to:**

- Enhance the accuracy of our eyes.

- Extend the observed vibration's spectral range beyond visible light.

We may do those as mentioned earlier by:

- Using and developing our peripheral vision.

- Increasing the amount of exposure.

- Improving visual sense processing in the brain — improving communication between the brain's left and right hemispheres.

Peripheral vision

What are the benefits of using your peripheral vision? The peripheral retina (the focus zone of the eye comprising photosensitive cells) is substantially more delicate than the central region. Because its precision is lower than that of the center region, humanity as a whole seems to be underutilizing the peripheral vision's potential. The center part of the retina is used mostly while reading, driving a vehicle, watching TV, and working on a computer. Because the center region of the retina is constantly in use, it accumulates damage over time from inappropriate and artificial lighting (TV, computers, artificial light).

Comprehension exercise 1

This exercise is meant to demonstrate how increasing exposure and utilizing peripheral vision may improve your eyesight— using vivid color highlighter pens, color all of the semicircle sections. Position the image 1.5 meters there next to you. For 30 seconds, focus your peripheral vision on the dark area and look for colored dots. Refrain from looking anyplace else than the dark spot.

The colored sections seem to be encircled by a different color's "Aura." When peripheral receptors are engaged for some time, we experience color sensations that are quite different from what we experience when we utilize our central vision. Because your sensitivity grows as you focus longer, the "Aura" surrounding colored spots becomes brighter. When you concentrate on the black area for an extended period, the "Aura" becomes almost as vivid as the original colors. You can view Auras around individuals if you can discern "Auras" of various colors surrounding colored places. This exercise shows the notion of perceiving auras rather than the actual aura.

Comprehension exercise 2

It is commonly known that the brain's opposing hemisphere evaluates each eye's vision. This exercise tries to improve communication between the brain's 2 hemispheres. Its task is to teach you how to utilize each eye independently and then merge the images in your brain. Use the colored circles to help you. Place the image around 1.5 meters next to you.

One of your fingers should be between and beneath the circles when you stretch your hand forward. Shift your attention to the touch of a finger and ignore the processes. There should be 4 circles visible. Then, attempt to overlap the 2 center circles to reveal a single circle with a cross on top in the center. The assumption that the left side of the brain (which is linked to the right eye) is interacting with the right side is shown by seeing the cross (connected to the left eye).

This activity has been proven to be very beneficial: Maintaining the cross for 5 minutes seems to double the Aura's energy and encourage self-healing.

The cross will float and seem unsteady at first. To get a perfect cross, play about with the distance between your finger and your eyes. After 3-5 minutes, you will see a substantial difference, especially without blinking.

Short bursts of intense focus seem to be more effective and efficient than prolonged bursts of concentration disrupted by lack of expertise. With repetition, you should eventually be able to establish and maintain the cross without using your finger. Using your peripheral vision, attempt to become conscious of the other 2 circles, as well as anything else around you while maintaining the cross. With your peripheral vision, you should be able to perceive auric colors surrounding the colored circles. You are ready to perceive and interpret auras when you can analyze your circumstances using your field of vision without losing the cross or your attention.

CHAPTER 19
WHAT IS ESP (EXTRASENSORY PERCEPTION)?

ESP is short for extrasensory perception. According to the Oxford dictionary, it is defined as "the supposed faculty of perceiving things by means other than the known senses, e.g., telepathy. The Oxford dictionary goes on to define telepathy as "the supposed communication of thoughts or ideas by means other than the known senses." ESP is what is commonly known as the "sixth sense." While this term has been made quite popular through the media, such as in the M. Night Shyamalan movie about a boy who can communicate with ghosts, it is most often associated with telepathy and the power to transmit messages via the mind. ESP doesn't have a fixed definition, and what it encapsulates varies among both proponents and skeptics alike. Joseph Banks Rhine, who we encountered earlier in our chapters on the history of remote viewing, as well as precognition, includes a variety of psychic abilities under the banner of ESP, including intuition (instinctive understanding), clairvoyance (a broad banner for a range of extrasensory abilities), psychometry (the ability to receive information about a person by coming into contact with an object associated with them), telepathy (the ability to read minds and send messages psychically), and even precognition and it's opposite, retrocognition (see chapter 6 for more information). Another term that is used to describe ESP is "second sight" which, according to Mariam Webster, includes both remote viewing and precognition.

While ESP is known to cover quite a broad range of different psychic abilities, it is most widely used as a synonym for telepathy, and for most of this chapter, we will be treating it as such. But first, we are going to dive into the history of ESP as a broader subject, which takes us back to some familiar figures, including J.B. Rhine, who as you may now have learned has had a hand in quite a broad range of parapsychological pursuits.

A Brief History of ESP

When it comes to ESP, it is difficult to trace an accurate history because ESP can be defined broadly or narrowly. The broad definition incorporates everything from remote viewing to precognition to distant healing, and a summary of those practices can be found in chapters 1, 6, and 7 respectively (chapter 1 includes the history of psychic power, and thus ESP, also). However, if we limit ESP to the practice of telepathy, as it often is, we get a clearer history. The term was first coined in 1882 by Frederic W.H. Myers, who was one of the founders of the Society for Psychical Research (or the SPR for short). The Society for Psychical Research was set up with the express purpose of investigating a variety of ESP phenomena, including the practice of remote viewing, but it is perhaps best known for its investigations of the power of telepathy. Myers himself published widely on ESP and the paranormal. In one such work,

titled 'Human Personality and Its Survival of Bodily Death', Myers described what he called the "subliminal self," which is the personality as distinct from the body. Myers believed that this subliminal self existed beyond the physical realm and would exist after death, and was part of the reason why he believed that parapsychological abilities, such as remote viewing, telepathy, and other forms of ESP were possible.

Telepathy and clairvoyance have been contested much more vigorously than any other kinds of ESP or parapsychological phenomena. Remote viewing has, for the most part, been left up to the proponents of parapsychology; this is evident, for example, in the case of the CIA and Project Stargate. During these experiments, which spanned several decades, the work of proving the reality and power of remote viewing was left up to the experimenters, the CIA, and the DIA. These people were all believers, and it was not until the 1990s that skeptics began to involve themselves in experiments to demonstrate that remote viewing is not real. Before that, the experiments proceeded unhindered, and it was mostly believers and proponents that were engaged in such experiments. When it comes to telepathy and clairvoyance, they are by far the most well-known, popular, and widely practiced and believed in forms of ESP and parapsychology. With this high level of interest and popularity among believers, there has been an inspired counter-movement against practices like telepathy and clairvoyance. From the late 19th century onwards, especially into the 20th century, most highly published experiments in telepathy and clairvoyance have been met with criticism and skepticism from scientists and journalists who don't believe in the powers of psychic energy and have sought to cast doubt on the veracity of the claims of adherents to these psychic practices.

The Society for Psychical Research conducted many experiments on telepathy in the late 19th century and early 20th century. One such experiment was conducted with 5 sisters who claimed to have psychic and telepathic powers, named Emily, Mary, Maud, Kathreen, and Alice. These experiments involved the sending of telepathic messages to one another across a room without making a sound or giving off any physical cues. Similar experiments were conducted with Douglas Blackburn and G.A. Smith. However, in both of these experiments, the experimental subjects (Blackburn, Smith, and the sisters) all later claimed that they had been using visual signals, such as blinking and sleight hand gestures, which brought the experiments into disrepute.

Gilbert Murray is another telepath who hosted many successful experiments in the 1910s and 1920s. These experiments involved the 'reading of kinds' as the experimenter would convey a message to one subject and then Murray would attempt to "read" the message from the experimental subject. There was a 36% success rate during these experiments, which was considered to be very successful by the experimenters and other proponents of telepathy at the time. Some have later claimed that these results might have been attained as a result of hyperesthesia, which is a heightened sense of stimuli — in this case, a heightened sense of hearing. Regardless, these experiments and the successful results are still held in high esteem by telepathy enthusiasts today.

In the 1920s, several telepathy experiments were conducted over the radio. One of these experiments was carried out by Victor James Woolley, a British parapsychologist, through the BBC's radio channels. In this experiment, one set of subjects had to focus on and think about several objects located in a particular office in London. Listeners of the radio station then had to try to tap into these other subjects psychically and try to figure out what they were focusing on. Nearly 25.000 submissions were made, but the results were inconclusive. The problem was that just about anybody listening to the radio station could submit an answer, but there was no way of demarcating regular members of the public from people who genuinely had psychic powers.

Upton Sinclair was very heavily involved in the study of telepathy throughout his life. Upton Sinclair is a very popular American writer, perhaps best known for his 1906 political novel, 'The Jungle.' He published widely throughout his life, in both fiction and non-fiction, but one overlooked aspect of his work is his writings on the paranormal and particularly on telepathy and other kinds of ESP. In 1930, he published a book about the power of telepathy titled 'Mental Radio: Does It Work, and How?'. In this book, Upton Sinclair experimented with his wife, Mary Craig Sinclair, whom he believed to have psychic powers, including telepathy. In these experiments, Upton would draw sketches and Mary would try to read his mind and replicate these sketches by herself. If Upton drew a basic sketch of a sailboat, the goal would be to have Mary draw the same image or at least an image very similar, with similar angles, shapes, layout, and so on. In total, there were 290 images drawn by Upton. From his estimation, 65 of Mary's replicated images were very similar to his own, and 155 were described as "partial successes" (for example, a drawing of a car might be replicated as a drawing of a house but with a similar shape and layout, similarly-sized windows, and so on). There were 70 failures also, meaning images that failed to replicate anything similar to what Upton had drawn.

J.B. Rhine, who you should now be familiar with from the

experiments he conducted that have been listed in other chapters (particularly his work on remote viewing, precognition, and retrocognition) also involved himself in long-distance telepathy experiments when he was involved with the Society for Psychical Research. Critics have contested the results of these experiments, but he and other proponents attest to their validity as evidence of the power and reality of telepathy.

In the 1930s, Harold Sherman and Hubert Wilkins conducted some experiments in which they attempted to read each other's minds. At the end of the day, they would relax and try to tap into one another's minds and memories. They would then write down in a recording diary what they believed the other person had seen and done that day. By the end of the experiment, they reported more than 60% of successful results.

Eduardo Balanovski and John G. Taylor conducted a series of experiments later in the 1970s. Unlike previous experiments, which began on a more "paranormal" grounding, the experiments of Balanovski and Taylor started with a very scientific hypothesis. They argued that there could be a genuinely scientific basis for telepathy and ESP within electromagnetic fields or EM fields. EM fields are a concept within classical physics (but not quantum physics), and they describe an electrodynamic energy field that is created by an acceleration of electrical charges. They theorized that there could be a scientific basis for telepathy in the manipulation of these electrodynamic energy fields, however, after conducting several experiments they eventually determined that there was no evidence for telepathic manipulation of EM fields. Despite the lack of successful results, these are very interesting experiments worthy of really serious study by students of parapsychology and telepathy, as it is one of the first times since the 19th century that observable scientific phenomena (in this case, physics) were relied on to invoke a hypothesis and potential theory of ESP and energy manipulation.

What Makes ESP Distinct from Remote Viewing?

ESP, when defined as telepathy (as opposed to the broader definition that includes remote viewing and other forms of parapsychological phenomena) is similar to remote viewing in many ways but is also quite different. The main way that it is distinct from remote viewing is definitional. To be telepathic or to engage your telepathic capabilities means to can read minds or transmit information from your mind to another person's mind, without the aid of any kind of visual or auditory cues. Remote viewing, on the other hand, is the transmission of information from a distant location to the 'seer', so that somebody located in one room of a building can see the layout of another room, another building, or even something located in another country or on another continent. It does not, strictly speaking, involve the unpacking of information from another person's mind. If you were to engage your remote viewing abilities to gauge the contents of a room in another building, and at the same time we're able to "read" the mental contents of a person's mind situated in that room, then this would be a combination of both remote viewing and telepathy or ESP. Such an act would be covered under the broad definition of ESP, but not ESP as telepathy, which only involves the reading of minds, and would certainly not be considered to be an act 137 of "pure" remote viewing," which involves viewing a scene or setting from a distance (without visual aid), but not the reading of mind or the mental transmission of unspoken messages and information.

What Are the Similarities Between ESP and Remote Viewing?

The similarities between ESP as telepathy and remote viewing are quite innumerable. This is even true after setting aside the broader definition of ESP to include remote viewing itself. Telepathy, by its very nature, is performed remotely, even if the distance is often not very far. This means that there is a greater similarity between telepathy and remote viewing than there is between precognition and remote viewing, for example. With precognition, the most common practice is to read what is in one's future (what card they are about to pull from a pack of Zener cards or playing cards, for example). This means that the events all take place in the mind of one individual. However, with telepathy, we are talking about one individual reading the mind of another individual or transmitting information or mental imagery to them. Even if the 2 individuals are in the same room – heck, even if there is a laying of hands involved, there is still some level of distance between the 2 minds which are transmitting the energy or information. Therefore, there is always a remote aspect to telepathy.

Various telepathic and ESP experiments have had a marked similarity to remote viewing. The most obvious example is the aforementioned experiments performed by Upton Sinclair and Mary Craig Sinclair. As a quick recap, in these experiments, Upton would draw a total of 290 images (on different occasions) that he would then attempt to telepathically transmit to Mary, who would draw her reconstruction. This resulted in 65 accurate replications, 155 "partial successes," and 70 failures. Because Upton drew the drawing first and then Mary attempted to replicate them, she could well have been remotely viewing the drawings rather than reading Upton's mind telepathically. In this experiment, and his work 'Mental Radio: Does It Work, and How?', he attributes to his wife the psychic power of telepathy, however, it does raise the question as to whether she was engaging in telepathy or rather the power of remote viewing, despite both experimenters being quite convinced that this was, in fact, a telepathic occurrence.

Finally, we must not forget the link forged by our friend J.B. Rhine. He worked with the Society for Psychical Research to conduct experiments in both telepathy and remote viewing, as well as other forms of psychical power and energy transmission. When he was conducting his experiments with telepathy, he engaged in what he described as "long-distance telepathy." By this point, the comparisons should be obvious. Long-distance telepathy involves, as the name suggests, telepathic energy transmission performed at long distances. Therefore, it either incorporates elements of remote viewing or is so similar that there is a very significant overlap that the student of both disciplines should take careful note of.

How Can ESP Be Used in Conjunction with Remote Viewing?

The aforementioned experiments by J.B. Rhine are the best example of the way that ESP and telepathy can be used in conjunction with remote viewing. As for practical applications, 2 friends who both practice telepathy but are separated by the oceans or simply live in different towns and countries can practice communicating over long distances using a combination of telepathy and remote viewing, and can then compare their results over the phone or via the internet to test out their accuracy. This should probably not be practiced until some basic abilities in both remote viewing and telepathy have been established, but beyond that, the possibilities are endless. It is a good idea to start close, maybe in the same room with eyes closed or backs turned to one another, before moving on to different rooms and eventually to other buildings. If either of you takes a holiday in another country, this will make for a good opportunity to put your skills to the test and try your hand at communicating telepathically at very long distances, especially after already establishing a vision of one another (or just one to the other, depending on who has the stronger psychic capabilities) using the psychic powers of long-distance remote viewing.

Means and Methodology

First, we will briefly talk through the steps on how to develop your telepathic capabilities, and then establish a simple practice of getting the basics down. Then we will move on to means and methods of using telepathy/ESP and remote viewing in conjunction with one another. It is important to establish some basic skills in telepathy and ESP before trying to combine them with remote viewing.

The best exercise we can do is one that utilizes the Zener cards and the associated practices and techniques. Whether you use Zener cards, playing cards, tarot cards, or whatever else is up to you. But I would use the Zener cards if you can get hold of some. They have been used for ESP and psychic purposes for close to a century now, and so by using them you are connecting yourself with a long tradition of paranormal and psychic practice and are therefore contributing to the practice using your experiments and abilities. They are also a favorite of J.B. Rhine, who worked closely with Karl Zener (the creator of the cards) on psychic experiments throughout his working life. J.B. Rhine was prominent in both experiments with telepathy and remote viewing, so it is good to utilize his preferred modes of practice if we aim to combine both into one single, solitary practice.

You must work with a friend when engaging in the practice of telepathic reading and communication. This is not necessary when you've already established your abilities (if you just want to read somebody's mind), but when you're just getting started, you need somebody who can confirm or deny whether or not your attempt worked. So first, find a practicing partner that is interested in developing their psychic awareness. Now find a quiet spot to practice, we're going to start by sitting in the same room as one another. Take your Zener cards (or your playing cards, or whatever you're using as a substitute), and sit at the opposite sides of the room. Turn your backs to one another so that you're facing the wall and cannot see each other – make sure there are no reflective surfaces where you could catch a glimpse of the other person and their card, including windows and mirrors. Now, one of you must take the cards and shuffle them well. Then you, or they, should pull up the top card and look at the front of it. They should scan all of the lines and angles on the card and focus on building up a replica as a mental image in their mind's eye. So far this might sound similar to the remote viewing exercises. But this is where it gets interesting. The person holding and scanning the card must now set the deck down and close their eyes. With their eyes shut tightly, they should re-visualize the card in their mind's eyes. Let's suppose it is you who is holding the card. You must now rebuild that mental image of the card's sign or symbol in your imagination. Make sure you build up a really good image of the card, with all shapes, lines, angles, curves, and colors replicated as identically as possible. Now is the time to project the image to your co-practitioner.

Imagine a beam of white light leaving your head and passing over to the other person. Visualize this beam of psychic energy as intensely as possible so that it goes from your head right into your friend's mind. Picture it as a kind of stream of energy, with the flow moving in one direction (away from you and toward the other person). Now picture the image that you wish to project to your friend flowing along this river of energy and entering the other person's head. Use all of your imagination and visualizing power to get this image across from your mind to theirs.

Now the other person needs to try to be open to the image to "receive" it. Although this should be the other person, this time around we are going to assume that you are the receiver just for the sake of instruction. You need to meet the other person's visualization so that you can have a kind of joint visualization that connects the mental energy that the other person is projecting and that you are receiving as a kind of psychic bridge from one person to the other. Now as you see this stream of mental energy, notice that the flow is moving in one direction, from the projector to you, the receiver. Now as you focus on this energy, notice that an obscure pattern or object is making its way out of the other person's head, into your direction. This will be difficult to make out at first, but see if you can notice any shapes, lines, angles, curves, or colors. Slowly start to build up this shape or pattern until you get a clear design that looks like one of the Zener cards shapes (or playing cards, tarot cards, or whatever sort of cards you chose to use). Write down or draw down what you see and then stop and meet back up with your friend in the middle of the room to discuss the results. If you were accurate, make a note of exactly what you both felt, and if not, make a note anyway. Now try again, either invoking those same feelings if you were accurate or trying to feel for a different sort of sensation if not. As always, it is important to keep a record of your results even if you feel you were entirely unsuccessful. It is important to know what feelings and sensations accompany this success or lack of so that you can replicate it (or vary it) in future experiments.

Now, we can move on to combining this practice of telepathy with remote viewing. However, it is first important to establish some positive results from your telepathic practice, otherwise, there is so much point in complicating matters with advanced practices if you still have not mastered the basics. And by the basics, I mean the fundamentals. "Basic" should not be misconstrued as simple or easy in this context. There is nothing simple about practicing telepathy, remote viewing, or any other discipline within the broader practices of ESP and parapsychology. We are practicing and experimenting with the fringes of known reality here, and a lot of what we are working with is almost completely unchartered territory. Consider how advanced science like chemistry is today. People have developed medicines that can cure diseases that once killed millions of people, likewise, people can make atom bombs that could wipe out a continent, and vehicles that can move at speeds that were unthinkable a century ago. However, to get to this point, just consider the journey that has so far been traversed, especially in its origins. A long time ago, alchemists struggled for centuries to find some kind of chemical source of gold and elixirs of life that would involve a simple combination of basic, easy-to-find ingredients. While they were not successful in these endeavors, minor breakthroughs lead to greater discoveries, that each successive experimenter built on the grounds of. In time, we managed to reach the complex and sophisticated science of chemistry that we have today.

Why do I say all of this? Because, given how early these experiments in telepathy and remote viewing are within human history, we could only be in the primitive phase right now, tinkering with things that we don't understand, groping in the dark, and seeking breakthroughs. So, while the steps that the practice involves might be "simple" in and of themselves, that does not mean that these breakthroughs that we seek are easy. Far from it, this is pioneering work that we are engaged in, and it should be treated as such.

Once we have mastered the art of telepathy, it is time to expand into a combination of telepathy and remote viewing. Here we will use J.B. Rhine's method of "long-distance telepathy." Start by continuing the previous experiment with the same friend, only this time, go into separate rooms of the house and communicate via the phone or internet (or shouting, if possible). Now, repeat the initial experiment that we discussed previously. If you are the sender, shuffle the cards and pick out one at random. Stare at it for a good minute and let your eyes and mind completely absorb it so that it's burned onto your retinas. Then, gently close your eyes. Relax all of your muscles and try to clear your mind. Now see the image from the card, whether it was a Zener card shape or some other image, and allow the image to intensify. See the color and shape solidify in front of you, and trace over each of the lines, curves, corners, and angles from top to bottom. Try to make the color "jump out" at you, focus on making it intense, even more so than the original card.

Now, once you have that image firm in your mind, focus on seeing that beam of light traverse out from the back of your head to the person in the next room. Picture it flowing like a great river that continues to grow in intensity. Make it glow with a brilliant bright light, as bright as the sun, and allow it to pass into the head of the receiver. Once this stream of energy is established and you have made it as strong and bright as possible, focus on seeing the image from the card leaving your head and travel slowly up this river of electromagnetic energy. See the image and shape in all its color pass down this stream of energy and then pass into the head of your co-practitioner. Make it as intense and as vibrant as you possibly can.

If you are the receiver, then similarly clear your mind and relax all of the muscles in your body, sitting in a comfortable and fixed position, such as the half-lotus. With eyes closed, imagine a great bright stream of energy entering the back of your head, pulsating forward from the next room and ultimately from the mind of the sender. Allow this beam of light and energy to intensify in color, brightness, and vibrancy. Now notice a shape begin to form in the distance, abstractly and obscurely at first, but with more force and clarity as it approaches you. Notice the shape, lines, colors, and angles that are present in the image. As it passes along this great line of energy, it should become clearer and stronger, and easier to grasp with your mental-visual capabilities. Make a record of what you see and consult with your co-practitioner once the session is over.

When you have made progress, simply repeat the experiment. First, start in a separate house (or perhaps, if you have outdoor space, have one person sit in the back garden or on the front porch. And again, once progress has been achieved, move further and further away. Ultimately, you want to be able to practice at as great a distance as possible, even if it means sitting in a park somewhere on the other side of town. If one of you has to leave town for any reason or is perhaps planning on taking a holiday to another country, this presents you with the best opportunity possible. Repeat the same exercise with the same success and, as always, record the results in your diary — whether successful or unsuccessful, it doesn't matter, as all of this information is important in the end.

In conclusion, ESP/telepathy is one of the best psychic abilities to combine with remote viewing. It lends itself to the same sort of exercises, practices, and insights as remote viewing, and is smooth and compatible when one is trying to combine the 2. The same sort of abilities that one needs to tap into to be a successful telepath is utilized in remote viewing, and the skills are quite easily transferable. A good and consistent practice of telepathy can be expanded by distance and in this way can easily incorporate all of the various elements of remote viewing and the basic tools of remote viewing practice, such as Zener cards, can easily be repurposed for telepathy and long-distance telepathy. Next, we will consider the overlap between astral projection, otherwise known as astral travel, and remote viewing, which also lends itself easily to a combined practice due to the inherent similarities between both disciplines.

CHAPTER 20
CRYSTALS: HOW CAN
CRYSTALS HELP PSYCHIC?

There are many ways crystals can help psychic individuals. There are certain minerals, such as salt, that work as a mental cleansing agent and can also clear negative energies from your home. They will also keep you grounded and prevent you from feeling any negative emotions. If you're still not convinced, try adding quartz crystal vibrations for increased focus and clarity of thought.

It has been used for centuries to help people reach spiritual enlightenment; their powers come from the stunningly unique shapes that make them easy to identify when placed by your bedside or in your pocket.

Faceted crystals can be used as jewelry and make great gifts because they're made to be pleasing to look at. It's possible to find faceted quartz crystal earrings or pendants, which are also a great decorative addition to your home.

It is traditional to place crystals in a circle during psychic readings and healing sessions; their formation is believed to create an energy field that stimulates the growth of psychic abilities. Setting up the perfect psychic circle is easy, all you need is to have the right stones or crystals.

Placing crystals at the psychic center of a room helps you focus more on what's important in your life and can help you tap into other worlds of knowledge. Crystals are believed to be able to connect to all 4 elements: earth, water, fire, and air. You can place crystals in your home according to the element that will help you reach specific goals.

Here are some examples:

- The energies of air are believed to be strongest when you sit by a fireplace or the rays of the sun.

- It is said that a mirror placed by the riverside can reflect the psychic energy of water and will make you heal faster. You can also place a moonstone under your pillow; it will remind you of the strong female spirit and make you more in touch with your feminine side.

- If you wish to use water as a psychic cleanser, place 3 blue tourmalines on top of each other into a bowl of water; allow it to sit for less than half an hour before using. You can also place a black tourmaline on top of your altar to ward off negative energy.

- If you wish to keep unwanted energies away from your home, choose an onyx and place it in a corner of the room where you spend the most time. Place it directly above the window where you will see it, as that is thought to be the best spot for the stone's healing powers.

- To clear your psychic mind and cleanse you of negative energies, place a moonstone under your pillow.

- If you wish to feel warm and safe, choose an amethyst or garnet and place it on your altar. These stones will also help you feel more secure in any situation.

- If you wish to grow spiritually, place a clear quartz crystal on top of your altar; its ability to stimulate psychic powers makes it a valuable addition to the psychic circle.

- To heighten your psychic powers, place an amethyst at the center of your altar. A fire opal also works well for clearing negative energy from your home and will make you feel safe and secure if you surround it with white candles or other protective items.

CHAPTER 21
WHAT IS CHANNELING?

Channeling is a type of paranormal psychic ability in which the psychically gifted can "channel" information, thoughts, or experiences into a medium, such as writing, painting, or drawing. The most famous channeler of this time is Dr. Brian Weiss with hundreds of books written on the subject and over 10 million sold worldwide. According to himself, he says he has been continuously channeling since childhood. He has learned it from his deceased father.

Canada is an interesting country in terms of the history of channeling. Many people may be surprised that a form of psychic ability is still being practiced today in Canada. A lot has changed not only socially and culturally, but also scientifically concerning the study of the paranormal in general. Dr. Brian Weiss is an example of this, a noted author and speaker on the subject of channeling, who both researches and practices the practice himself.

Recently, there has been much controversy surrounding Dr. Weiss as many who have read his books have found that many of his theories about channeling are unsubstantiated or completely false. This is a point of contention in itself and goes to show that there are many unanswered questions about the practice itself. What is channeling and how exactly does it work? Who channels information, how is it done, and are the channels themselves reliable? Furthermore, what type of information can be channeled?

Dr. Brian Weiss explains: "I have learned from my father, who is still alive, to put words on paper." Weiss continues: "He was a very good pianist and he spoke about words I had written down for me at the piano where he would tune them. He has been practicing the art of channeling for nearly 40 years and many people had not heard of it before.

Brian Weiss was featured in a recent article in the National Post, "I Am Not a Fraud," by author Aaron Hutchins, who is also a very well-known skeptic of Dr. Weiss. Many interesting facts were brought to light during Hutchins' investigation into Dr. Weiss' activities as he had previously said "I would say that I channel messages on one-third of my channeled messages." These facts call into question whether or not he is truly a fraud.

In a recent interview with Project Camelot, Brian Weiss discusses his skepticism concerning extraterrestrial channeling, which he has done on numerous occasions, as he claims that many of the messages were from extraterrestrial sources. These messages were channeled via psychic children who claimed to have been contacted by extraterrestrials and Dr. Weiss himself admits that some of the information was false.

CHAPTER 22
CLAIRVOYANCE, CLAIRAUDIENCE, CLAIRSENTIENCE AND CLAIRCOGNIZANCE

Intuition can be defined as the individual's ability to have or obtain express knowledge or sudden insight without reasoning, observations, or thinking. People place enough importance on their gut feelings when making unfamiliar decisions. Such instinctive feelings are what intuition is all about. Your instinct guides you when going through uncertainty or charting a new course that seems to be against all available evidence.

Intuition plays a crucial role in management, sports, relationships, and entrepreneurship, where one is forced to make decisions with uncertain outcomes. In such situations, intuition is what we turn to guide us, hopefully for the desired result. There are 4 kinds of intuition that a psychic empath can obtain:

1. Clairvoyance

It means clear seeing. With this form of intuitive ability, you see things clearly in your mind as pictures, symbols, short moving images, or impressions. Of the 4 intuitive abilities, this is the most visual. The psychic can perceive sudden images, either in black and white or color. They can be impressions that form a vision in your mind's eye. People with intuitive clairvoyance ability often have vivid or lucid dreams which are caused by their awakened intuition.

2. Clairaudience

It means clear hearing. With this intuitive ability, the psychic hears information inside his or her mind. This information is received as words, or also as a song lyric, sound, or even a faraway vibration. Among all intuition types, this is considered the easiest to occur (and often mistaken for hearing disturbances). People with this type of ability are called clairaudients, and when this phenomenon happens, they usually perceive a light pressure around an area situated below their temples but above the ears, while they receive the information.

3. Clairsentience

A very common kind of intuition can also be clairsentience. It is when you feel something is going to happen. If you've ever heard someone, use the phrase "I can just feel it" or "this doesn't feel right," these are signs of clairsentience. It is what you often call your "gut feeling" or your instinct. This instinct is very common among empaths because it amplifies their ability to sense others' emotions. Maybe you feel a wave of sadness before your friend walks into a room, and then they tell you their mother has passed away. Maybe you're on the phone with your friend who has a broken right leg, and you feel a brief pain in your right leg, even before knowing about their injury. Maybe you see your pet and suddenly burst into tears, overwhelmed by sadness for no apparent reason, and within a week, the pet dies.

4. Claircognizance

It is when your intuition helps you figure something out that your rational brain can't, something you're maybe stuck on. For example, if you're stuck in traffic, should you risk taking the upcoming exit to get out of it and take the backroad, or will that end up taking longer? You inexplicably decide to wait it out, and soon traffic has cleared, and you're on your way. This is claircognizance. If you've ever heard someone, say, "I just know," and they don't have evidence to prove their certainty or no way of knowing, but end up being right—that is claircognizance.

CHAPTER 23
LUCID DREAMS

A lucid dream is different from astral travel, but it can project the soul outward of the body for astral travel. By definition, lucid dreams are dreams that dreamers are aware of. In lucid dreaming, a person has already achieved the out-of-body experience.

Since lucid dreaming is a good way to achieve astral projection, you must first become obsessed with the out-of-body experience. As soon as your mind is filled with the thoughts and ideas of out-of-body experience, you must give your mind affirmations of lucid dreaming by reminding yourself all day long. This is to program your subconscious mind to induce lucid dreaming once you close your eyes at night time.

Displaced Awareness Technique

This is another technique that can help you train yourself to do astral projection. With this technique, close your eyes and start to get into a trans-state. Once you get into the trance state, try to get a sense of the entire room. Feel your head above your shoulders but be very passive about the things that are going on around you. You need to observe what is happening around you and accept everything that's going on around you.

Imagine that your astral body is rotating 180 degrees. As soon as you finish your mental rotation, the position of your astral body should change. This means that your astral head needs to be where your physical feet used to be and vice versa. With this new picture in your mind, visualize the room in a new direction. This is the reason why it is called the displaced awareness technique.

When you get displaced to a new position, you will eventually feel dizzy because of the direction change. This is a normal sensation and you should not be afraid of it. Once you get comfortable with the new position, imagine yourself floating slowly to the roof. You will feel yourself "popping" out of your physical body.

Jump Technique

This technique is a great way to do astral travel from dreams. It is a technique wherein you can wake up from your dreams and subject yourself to a lucid state. To make this technique work, you need to ask yourself whether you are dreaming or not. The thing is that there are times when you are not aware of whether you are already dreaming or in a waking state. To verify that you are dreaming, you need to jump as though you are going to fly. If you are awake and in your physical body, you will eventually land on the ground with a great big thump. If you are dreaming, then you can defy gravity and end up floating.

Once you realize that you are dreaming, you can eventually transform your dream into lucid dreaming so that you can finally go through an out-of-body experience.

Thirst Technique

Designed by Sylvan Muldoon, the thirst technique is considered one of the most pleasant and effective of all astral projection techniques. To do this technique, you need to refrain from drinking hours before you go to bed. Instead, increase your thirst throughout the day by reducing your water intake. However, keep a glass of water in front of you and start at it. Imagine drinking the water but resisting the temptation to do so.

Before sleeping, eat a pinch of salt and place the glass of water at a convenient place away from the bed as you practice in your mind the actions to do astral projection. Get up and cross the room to reach the glass, then go to bed while still thinking about your thirst. Go to sleep. At night, you might be awakened in your dream and find yourself walking toward the glass of water. This is your sign that you are having an out-of-body experience. Make sure that you take note of the sensations that you feel.

Stretch Out Technique

This is also an easy technique that can help you achieve astral projection. To do this method, lie down and shut your eyes. Make sure that your body is relaxed. Then, imagine your feet stretching out and getting longer. Hold on to this picture and eventually let your feet go back to normal. Now, do the same thing for your head. Eventually, you will feel dizzy while doing the astral stretching exercise. The floating sensation is your signal that you can pull your soul out of your body to do astral travel.

Hammock Technique

As the name implies, this technique suggests that you imagine yourself on a white hammock located in a secluded and peaceful place. While lying on the hammock, imagine your hammock swaying in the wind. Repeat this visualization until you feel relaxed. Like the other astral projection techniques, you will also feel varying intensities of vibrations in your body. Once you feel the vibrations with this technique, you can roll out of your body to undergo an out-of-body experience.

CHAPTER 24
GHOSTBUSTING

Ghostbusting is a paranormal investigation technique that involves gathering empirical evidence to account for possible ghostly apparitions by using one or more of the 5 senses.

Some also involve multiple investigators and/or use electronic equipment like video cameras and motion detectors.

The objective of ghostbusting is to determine the credibility of an alleged haunting by collecting data that can be used to assess different aspects of the events in question, such as whether or not it would be possible for a spirit to produce an effect without a physical presence.

It is similar to criminal investigation in that evidence, such as data and recordings, either support or refute the credibility of claims.

The instruments like flashlights, night vision equipment, infra-red cameras, and thermal imaging cameras enhance their abilities to capture various types of activities. Therefore, ghostbusting depends on the impartial collection and analysis of data for a case by a group or individual.

Scientists who study the evidence produced by ghost hunters are skeptical. Their skepticism is mainly based on the extreme likelihood of fraud and methodological flaws. The field of paranormal research is criticized for lacking scientific methods, as it does not have strict protocols for testing beliefs about ghosts or even a clear understanding of what a ghost is, which leaves any results open to doubt and scrutiny.

There has never been a universally recognized, academically researched, and tested professional standard reference work that sets an objective analysis and classification of alleged spirit encounters.

Some critics consider ghostbusting to be "pseudoscience," while others believe it can be treated as an experimental science until it can be proven, otherwise, by mainstream science.

Ghostbusters are considered to be amateur investigators. Many ghost hunters are men and women who have seen one too many horror films that have frightened them into believing that they need to test their bravery against the unknown.

Video cameras, motion sensors, thermal imagers, etc. Ghostbusting is a bit simpler and can be done by just about anyone. The equipment used for ghost hunting is expensive while ghostbusting gear can be found in local hardware stores sold under "ghost hunting supplies." Ghost hunters generally do not differentiate between hauntings and poltergeist activity. They gather evidence of their findings in an attempt to prove 162 the existence of ghosts. Ghostbusters, on the other hand, do not necessarily believe that ghosts exist in the first place and therefore all evidence gathered is either a natural occurrence, the result of an error, or fraud.

Thus, ghostbusting is a test of one's ability to determine the difference between reliable evidence and hoaxes.

As a result, ghostbusters will often spend a lot more time trying to find natural explanations for observed phenomena. This may include researching past events in the place's history, previous owners, incidents of death or other tragedies, and abnormalities on maps, such as magnetic fields and energy vortices.

Determine if paranormal activity is taking place in a given location by examining evidence gathered at different times, as well as from different witnesses. This enables the ghostbuster(s) to rule out eyewitnesses that are prone to misinterpretation or misperception.

The alleged haunting is, in fact, attention-seeking behavior by any witnesses or hoaxing by the spectators and/or investigators.

Understanding various aspects of the paranormal, such as alleged ghostly apparitions that have led to the development of various theories about them.

CHAPTER 25
MEDIUM

Mediumship or mediums may be a term you have not heard before. As mentioned above, a medium is a person who is a bridge between the dead and the living. They can communicate with those who have passed away and relay messages to the living for them. If you have ever used an Ouija board, this is a form of mediumship, as you are contacting, or attempting to contact, the spirits of the dead, although Ouija boards are usually used as a form of entertainment rather than as something serious.

The forms of mediumship used by practicing mediums are when the spirit of the dead speaks through the medium, and when the medium receives messages clairvoyantly (or clairsentient, claircognizant, clairaudient) and relays the message to the living. Most of the time, the medium is requested by a living person to try to contact and create a channel of communication with a deceased loved one because they miss them and/or because there are unfinished businesses or unanswered questions between them and they want a sense of closure. The spirit of the deceased loved one probably feels the same way, so these sessions can be very healing.

If you wish to become a medium, an intermediary between the spirit world and the living, you will need to have a strong command of all four types of intuition (even if you favor one more than the others), as messages will come to you and you will perceive them through clairvoyance, clairaudience, clairsentience or claircognizance. This is something you should try once you have practiced your psychic abilities for a while and feel confident. You can continue on the beginner's path, but make sure you have the basics down. If you feel that you are a natural medium, someone who has felt the presence of the spirits of the dead from a young age, then you may already have an idea of how to communicate and use these spiritual channels. However, this is not a necessity for becoming a medium.

Numerology refers to the study of how numbers are related to people, events, and ideas. Each number is said to have a specific meaning that relates to its number value on different levels: spiritual, mental, emotional, or physical, which can be learned more about from various websites and books. For example, 9/11 meanings could be used with both 3/9, as well as 9/11 values in numerology.

Numerological interpretation can be used as a form of divination, which means "to foresee through numbers." The principle behind numerology might be considered similar to Kabbalah's concept of Chokmah (intellect). Numerology can also be used to assign personality traits based on numbers.

Associated with the occult, even though many people have a talent for it, numerous institutions and companies offer numerological services. Numerologists use a combination of astrology and numerology to form a personal meaning for life events, especially birth dates although numerology can also be applied to other areas of life, such as money or personality traits. There are certain styles or schools of numerology depending on how particular techniques and interpretations are combined by the practitioner.

It is not the same as a statistical methodology, which deals with numbers in terms of probability. A well-known application of numerology used by some is to determine the compatibility of new couples in a relationship. This can be done with their birth dates, and numerologists may make predictions about how an individual's personality or relationships will change or progress over time.

The concept of Numerology was used by John Dee, would-be astrologer to Queen Elizabeth I through his first wife Mary Brydges, and later Dee's second wife, Francisco most likely a circle member.

Has been studied and written about in Homer's Iliad, several of the Old Testament books of the Bible, as well as Chinese writings from around 500 B.C. (Kjellman). Before Numbers can be manipulated, they must be converted into their single digits (Arabic numerals) first then many different styles or methods are used to assess that number.

There are 2 basic kinds of numerology systems — those based on the meanings of numbers and those based on their numerical values. Meaning-based numerology is most often associated with Pythagoreanism because its founder, Pythagoras (sixth century BC), ascribed meanings to 1 through 9. It has been suggested that the Pythagoreans added the 10th number to the list of sacred numbers and its position in the list was changed after Pythagoras' death.

In the second meaning-based tradition of number study, which is also called Numerology or Gematria (from the Greek word for 'number'), each of the numbers 1 through 9 has a specific symbolic meaning, assigned by God at creation. The purpose of this system is to facilitate understanding and truth-seeking because numbers don't have gender, race, or other such qualities that could be considered negative. The numbers are representative of spiritual truths and their numerical values can be used to determine a person's traits, behaviors, and problems.

Morgan was known as the "father of Numerology" in 1781 AD. He studied the Quran, and books of occult and numerology to conclude that a system that uses numbers for divination should be created. He also translated the Vedas and learned from them. Morgan's system was based on Pythagorean influences, as well as other systems he had been exposed to from around the world.

John Hawkins, who made numerology popular in England in 1887 AD, studied under William Wollstonecraft. He also studied Ouija boards and corresponded with Arthur Edward Waite until 1891 AD when he founded his school (1899) in Liverpool. He wrote the book 'Numerology' and is the source of most "facts" in numerology. He said that numbers have qualities and meanings and that they affect human lives while a person is being born. Hawkins used Pythagorean numerology, like Morgan.

Alfred Charles Viper was a deaf mason who created his system based on Pythagorean tradition but added to it more than 100 meanings for each number using an array of medieval legends, mythology, and historical figures. His main focus was on religion in general for which he amassed a great deal of interesting data about biblical characters and their names (from the Old Testament). He continued the tradition of Ouija boards, which he learned from friends, who were also deaf. Viper's work was a huge contribution to the field of numerology, for he made it more popular among other occultists.

In the 1980s and 1990s, numerology became increasingly popular with the New Age movement. Numerology has also had a long history in the Jewish Kabbalah and has been used by Christians since antiquity; Dante's Divine Comedy is written in terza rima and contains 9 circles of hell (Inferno 9).

Numerology is now used extensively by psychics, who claim that they can interpret one's destiny. Numerologists also use computers. In the early years of computer programming, John Vincent Atanasoff and others used numerology to assign binary values to the letters of the alphabet to create programming languages.

A number represents a person's potential, their personality and has many different meanings for different people. Many parts of one's life are based on numbers, such as age, date of birth, time of birth, address, and telephone number.

Deciphering a person's potential is not as simple as adding up their numbers or counting. The meaning of a number is determined by the numbers surrounding it. This is referred to as its 'vibration'. For each number, there are 2 main forms of vibration; a personal vibration for an individual and an expression vibration for the world. The difference between the final number in a person's name and their birth date is the most common form of numerology.

After one reaches 8 years of age, it is believed that their brain finishes its development and it is believed that they will be more 'mature' and will have fewer tantrums. If a person is born in one of these months, it is believed that they will absorb the qualities associated with that month.

The second step to take is to examine the day of the month. In numerology, there are also 28 separate personality traits, each one linked to a specific letter of the alphabet. These letters can be found in our names or birthdates.

CHAPTER 26
TELEPATHY

Telepathy is one of the most powerful psychic abilities in which it enables the psychic to send and receive thoughts or feelings from another person using only the power of the mind without using any physical interactions. Users of this psychic ability are often called "mind readers" or "telepaths." Telepathy can be categorized into 2 kinds: Telepathic Communication, which is the ability to send thoughts and feelings using the psychic's mind into another psychic's mind, and Telepathic Perception, which is the ability to receive thoughts and feelings using the psychic's mind from another psychic's mind. There are 3 major types of telepathy: Instinctual Telepathy, Dream Telepathy, and Mental Telepathy.

Instinctual Telepathy

This is the type of telepathy that most of us have, it is when a psychic senses the feelings or needs of someone that is nearby via a mental connection. It uses the area around our solar plexus which is the center of our instincts and emotions. This is where the term "gut feel" came from. This type of telepathy is something that we often experience with people with whom we have a strong emotional and mental attachment, such as our loved ones, parents, spouse, siblings, or very close friends. The most noticeable example of instinctual telepathy involves sensing intense emotions when someone is in an emergency, serious distress, or death.

Dream Telepathy

This is the type of telepathy that occurs when a psychic communicates with someone's mind or receives a telepathic transmission while being in a dream. An example of this is when you have a dream about someone close to you being sad and attempting to overdose himself with sleeping pills while, indeed, it is happening in real life or is about to happen. This is a sign of telepathic transmission that you have received by having insights into that someone's mind. Another example is when you meet a friend in your dream and you tell them something then when you wake up and meet that person in real life, you both had the same dream and he received your message. You might think that it is a coincidence but that is a sign that you sent a telepathic transmission to your friend.

Psychological Telepathy

This is the hardest type of telepathy to perform because it requires a lot of practice and dedication. Psychological telepathy is the direct transmission of information from the psychic's mind to another mind. While most humans and animals have instinctual telepathy, this extrasensory perception requires the opening of our "third eye" which opens up the mind to the world beyond our 5 senses. The third eye is the center of telepathy and other psychic abilities. The main difference between instinctual and psychological telepathy is that the first one occurs naturally and sometimes without even us noticing while the second one is intentional.

How to Practice and Develop Your Telepathic Abilities

If you want to develop your telepathic abilities, it would require consistent practice and the following steps:

1. Believe in yourself and believe in telepathy

The first step toward telepathic communication is to believe in yourself and that telepathy exists. Remove all the doubts in your heart and mind and surrender yourself to the powers of your third eye.

2. Find a willing partner with whom you have strong bonds

Find someone with whom you have strong bonds and have an open mind who also believes in telepathy. If one of you has doubts, you may have a hard time achieving mental communication. Your partner can be a close friend, your spouse, or one of your family members.

3. Focus your thoughts

The first step is to relax your body and mind before focusing on your thoughts. Find a comfortable position and start to meditate. Tell your partner to also do the same to receive your telepathic transmission.

4. Imagine the person you are communicating with

The next thing to do while you are focused is to imagine the person you are trying to communicate with telepathically. Close your eyes and try to picture your partner and every detail about him as close as you possibly can like the way he looks, how tall he is, and every specific detail that you can visualize.

5. Visualize the message you are trying to send

After Imagining that the person you are trying to communicate telepathically with is in front of you, you should visualize the message you are trying to send. You can start with a simple object like a pen, try to visualize it as detailed as possible, and focus your mind only on it. Imagine the object's shape, size, color, weight, length, and all the other characteristics that you can imagine and transmit that mental image to your telepathic partner.

6. Tell the receiver to write down what came to their mind

After you have sent the telepathic message you are trying to send, your partner should remain calm and focused until they feel that the thought has entered their mind. Then, you should ask them to write down what is the thought that came to their mind in complete detail. You should also write the message you are trying to send your partner.

7. Compare the results

After both write the thought, try to compare your results and see if both have the same things you have written down. At first, you may not be successful but do not get discouraged because with practice you will soon be able to communicate telepathically. Just try again and practice until you can consistently tell what each other is thinking about.

How Can You Tell the Difference BetweenTelepathy and Imagination?

Finding the difference between telepathy and imagination is as simple as creating an experiment with your telepathy partner. You can also confirm if your vision is telepathy or imagination by asking the people involved in your vision. For example, when you suddenly saw a picture in your mind that shows your spouse in a dangerous situation. You should definitely call her immediately and ask her to confirm but do not suddenly ask her questions that will freak her out like "Did you have an accident, are you okay?" Instead, you can ask her for other specific details that can be connected to your vision like "Where are you right now?" or "What are you currently doing?" After that, you can compare her answers if it is connected to the vision you saw.

Do not worry because you will only be confused about it in the beginning. Once you get comfortable with your ability you will be able to tell right away if it is just your imagination or it is a telepathic transmission.

CONCLUSION

In conclusion, psychic and empath abilities are common throughout the world, but not so much that it is abnormal not to have them. With this said, if you do have one or both of these abilities and need someone to talk to about any related concerns, contact a mental health professional or an organization like the Association for Psychical Research. Remember that with each person's experience comes an individual reaction and treatment plan.

Discussing a mental health issue with a practitioner, simply let the person know you want to resolve the matter and allow them to help. Please! Provide as much detail as you can until you obtain a resolution. If you are unable to discuss this topic in person or over the phone, then send an email or letter asking for feedback and any assistance they can provide.

Clairvoyance is the ability to see things at a distance. It can be seen in many everyday instances. Everyone has experienced clairvoyance, even if he or she does not know it. For example, have you ever known someone who didn't feel well and predicted they were getting sick? Have you ever been somewhere that made you feel uneasy without knowing why? This is clairvoyance.

Empaths are people with the ability to read other individuals' emotions and feelings. Some may possess the ability to do this for all people, but others can read just one individual's feelings.

They can predict and detect other people's emotions without knowing. This is also called "precognition."

Made in the USA
Monee, IL
25 November 2022

18459557R00098